*f*P

# We're All Journalists Now

The Transformation of the Press and
Reshaping of the Law in the Internet Age

## SCOTT GANT

FREE PRESS
*New York   London   Toronto   Sydney*

FREE PRESS
A Division of Simon & Schuster, Inc.
1230 Avenue of the Americas
New York, NY 10020

First Free Press hardcover edition June 2007

FREE PRESS and colophon are trademarks of
Simon & Schuster, Inc.

For information about special discounts for bulk purchases,
please contact Simon & Schuster Special Sales at
1-800-456-6798 or business@simonandschuster.com

Designed by Kyoko Watanabe

Manufactured in the United States of America

1   3   5   7   9   10   8   6   4   2

Library of Congress Cataloging-in-Publication Data
is available.

ISBN-13: 978-0-7432-9927-5

*To my teachers,*
*inside and outside the classroom,*
*for instilling a love of ideas*

# Contents

# We're All
# Journalists Now

# CHAPTER ONE

# We're All Journalists Now

---

The pantheon of modern American journalists is occupied by familiar names, like Bob Woodward and Carl Bernstein, Walter Cronkite, Mike Wallace, Rush Limbaugh, Bill O'Reilly. Wait a minute . . . Rush Limbaugh? Bill O'Reilly? Yes, according to a poll conducted in 2005, 40 percent of respondents identified Bill O'Reilly as a journalist, while only 30 percent said the same of Bob Woodward—slightly more than Rush Limbaugh's 27 percent.

Perhaps these results should not be surprising. After

all, what is a journalist? What differentiates journalists from other people disseminating ideas and information to the public? Today, the answer is hardly self-evident, and depends very much on whom you ask.

The most recent edition of the *New Oxford American Dictionary,* published in 2005, defines journalism as the "activity or profession of writing for *newspapers* or *magazines* or of broadcasting news on *radio* or *television.*" The focus on these four specific vehicles for communication suggests the dictionary is somewhat behind the times, but it raises broader questions about whether limiting the concept of journalism to certain media makes any sense. Why should we include broadcast television, but exclude a DVD of a documentary watched on the same television monitor? Why should newspapers and magazines qualify, but not books?

The dictionary's definition also does not get us far, since it is hardly clear what qualifies as "news." What about editorials and opinion pieces? If they do not qualify as journalism, why not? If they do, then what about opinions expressed in pamphlets, in newsletters, or on Web sites?

Does whether someone is considered a journalist depend on where his or her words are published? On whether he gets paid? On whether she offers only "objective" facts or also supplies her own analysis and ideas?

It was not long ago that the boundaries between

journalists and the rest of us seemed relatively clear. Those who worked for established "news organizations" were journalists; everyone else was not. In the view of most, you knew the press when you saw it.

Those days are gone. The lines distinguishing professional journalists from other people who disseminate information, ideas, and opinions to a wide audience have been blurred, perhaps beyond recognition, by forces both inside and outside the media themselves. Whatever the causes, it is harder than ever to tell who is a journalist.

The implications of this predicament are important. The question arises routinely in American courtrooms and legislatures, and at other government institutions, because there are many circumstances where those deemed "journalists" are afforded rights and privileges not available to their fellow citizens.

As with many areas of our lives, the legal system plays a central role in determining how information is collected and disseminated; who gets access to information, and when, and how; and whether someone has the right to keep information to himself, or may be compelled to divulge it. A mixture of provisions in the federal and state constitutions, statutes, regulations, and court decisions serves as the rulebook for how we communicate as a society. Unfortunately, when it comes to figuring out who is a journalist, and whether professional journalists are entitled to rights and privileges beyond those enjoyed by others, the rulebook is a mess.

But the problem extends beyond mere confusion. Although the federal courts have not (at least so far) interpreted the Constitution as distinguishing between professional or institutional journalists and other citizens, many government officials (including some judges) nonetheless adhere to the idea that traditional journalists should be afforded rights and privileges not available to others—an idea championed by most established media organizations and many professional journalists.

For example, the District of Columbia and virtually every state have, through statutes or court decisions, established some variety of "privilege" for journalists, often referred to as a "shield law." Although the contours of the privilege vary by jurisdiction, in general they exempt those identified as journalists from having to disclose information they would be forced to reveal were they ordinary citizens—such as the identity of a source.

Congress has yet to enact a federal shield law. It is currently considering whether to do so, prompted in part by the criminal investigation led by Department of Justice special counsel Patrick Fitzgerald, arising from the well-publicized "outing" of then–CIA operative Valerie Plame Wilson, in which several reporters were compelled to identify their sources to prosecutors because of the absence of such a law. Among those reporters was the *New York Times*'s Judith Miller, who spent eighty-five days in prison for her refusal.

Yet even without a federal shield law, the national government has scores of rules and regulations that favor professional journalists over others. These include: Department of Justice guidelines that impose higher standards for subpoenaing "members of the news media" than other citizens; federal regulations that limit or prohibit travel to certain foreign countries (such as Iraq) but exempt "*recognized* newsgathering organizations"; and even the Supreme Court's own rules that for years permitted no audience members other than journalists credentialed by the Court to take notes during oral argument.

Although many thoughtful observers embrace the view that professional journalists should be routinely afforded rights and privileges unavailable to others, I believe it is misguided. The circumstances in which it is necessary and justifiable to extend preferential treatment only to them are few. We should no longer accept the routine extension of special perks and protections to professional journalists that are denied to others seeking to engage in essentially the same activities. The First Amendment is for all of us—and not just as passive recipients of what the institutional press has to offer.

"Freedom of the press is guaranteed only to those who own one," remarked A. J. Liebling, the acclaimed *New Yorker* writer, many decades ago. Yet with the advent of the Internet and the World Wide Web, Liebling's otherwise astute observation seems profoundly dated. Inexpensive and powerful personal computers and software now enable almost everyone to easily share information and opinions with a global audience.

These technological advances are converging with a series of social and economic forces to transform journalism. This transformation should help bring into focus a reality we somehow lost sight of— that journalism is an endeavor, not a job title; it is defined by activity, not by how one makes a living, or the quality of one's work. Although we are not all engaged in the *practice* of journalism, any one of us can be if we want to. In that respect, we're *all* journalists now.

## Journalism in Transition

Journalism is in flux. Most newspapers and magazines face dwindling readership and the loss of advertisers (including highly profitable classified advertisements) as they compete with electronic publications and other sources of information and entertainment. Television news similarly struggles for viewers and for its self-identity, in a largely unsuccessful pursuit of ratings and profits.

At the same time, journalists are confronting a spate of high-profile efforts to compel the disclosure of confidential sources—displacing the threat of libel lawsuits as the main legal preoccupation of many news organizations. For instance, in 2006, *New York Times* reporters were forced to provide prosecutors probing the leak of information related to an investigation of two Islamic charities with their phone records. Around the same time, two *San Francisco Chronicle* reporters were held in contempt of court and ordered to spend up to 18 months in jail for failing to reveal who provided them with secret grand jury testimony about alleged steroid use by a number of professional athletes (the reporters' jail sentences were suspended while they appealed, and later lifted when, during the appeals process, their apparent source—whom they still will not identify—pleaded guilty to several federal offenses related to leaking the grand jury testimony).

Meanwhile, the investigation into the disclosure of Valerie Plame's work for the CIA also led to the indictment (and subsequent conviction) of Vice President Cheney's former chief of staff, Scooter Libby, on charges of perjury and obstruction of justice. Not only were prosecutors able to obtain confidential information from reporters during their investigation of the revelation about Plame, but the subsequent trial of Libby resulted in the forced disclosure of information by journalists to Libby's defense team, and ultimately to the appearance of ten journalists as witnesses during the trial itself.

But the recent wave of subpoenas is not limited to high-profile cases or news organizations in major media markets. A reporter at the *Wilkes-Barre Times Leader* in Pennsylvania received at least three subpoenas seeking information about his interviews with a murder suspect. In Rhode Island, a judge refused to nullify a subpoena issued to a reporter from the *Westerly Sun*, a small newspaper serving Rhode Island and southeast Connecticut. In Mankato, Minnesota, a judge ordered a reporter from that city's *Free Press* to turn over his notes from a phone interview conducted with a man in the midst of a standoff with local police, which ended when the man apparently took his own life.

Nor are these efforts limited to criminal proceedings. It appears that in an increasing number of civil lawsuits (which do not involve alleged violations of criminal laws) courts are enforcing requests by private parties to compel the disclosure by journalists of information relevant to the case. One high-profile example is the lawsuit filed by former government scientist Steven Hatfill against the *New York Times* and its columnist Nicholas Kristof, in which Hatfill alleged he was defamed in several Kristof columns examining who might be responsible for a series of lethal anthrax attacks in late 2001. After the court in that case ordered the *Times* to identify Kristof's sources for the columns, it named some (who apparently released Kristof from his confidentiality pledge) but refused to identify others, leading the court to preclude the *Times* from using information provided by those unidentified sources when defending itself at trial. The court, however, subsequently ruled in favor of the *Times* and dismissed the case before submitting it to a jury—a ruling Hatfill is appealing.

Another well-publicized recent example is a lawsuit by Wen Ho Lee, a former Department of Energy scientist, investigated on suspicion of spying for China (an offense with which he ultimately was not charged), who filed a claim against the government under a statute called the Privacy Act, based on the alleged leaking of his confidential personal information by the agency. Lee sought the testimony of several journalists who had written stories about him, in an effort to learn who in the government might have provided them with information.

Efforts by the journalists to convince two courts that they should not have to reveal the information sought by Lee were unsuccessful, and they were held in contempt for their refusal. The journalists—and the news organizations for which they worked—asked the Supreme Court of the United States to hear their case. While that request was pending (the Court is not required to hear all of the cases in which review is sought), Lee's lawsuit was settled on remarkable terms. The government agreed to pay $895,000, with the proviso that the money not go to Lee himself—it could be used only to pay his attorneys, for litigation expenses, and for taxes owed on the settlement funds. In addition, to the astonishment of almost everyone, as part of the deal under which Lee would drop his case, five media organizations whose reporters were being pursued as witnesses agreed to pay him $750,000. The organizations—ABC News, the Associated Press, the *Los Angeles Times*, the *New York Times*, and the *Washington Post*—released a joint statement explaining that they reluctantly paid the money to protect their confidential sources and shield their reporters from possible imprisonment. CNN, which had also covered the Lee story and whose reporter was targeted as a witness, refused to participate in the settlement, stating that "we had a philosophical disagreement over whether it was appropriate to pay money to Wen Ho Lee or anyone to get out from under a subpoena."

The payment by media organizations to settle a case in which they were not defendants appears unprecedented—and stirred debate within journalism circles. It also reflects growing concern among traditional news organizations that they are losing standing with the public and with the judiciary. Polls consistently reflect public dissatisfaction with the press. Recent rejections of media organizations' claims that they should be exempt from laws applicable to other citizens have left the press increasingly worried about how they will fare in the courts. "We've seen greater skepticism on the part of the judiciary," which doesn't "seem to see the role of the press as uniquely contributing to our democratic process," acknowledges Jane Kirtley, the longtime director of the Reporters Committee for Freedom of the Press, and now a professor at the University of Minnesota's School of Journalism and Mass Communication. As a result, traditional media organizations are rethinking their newsgathering methods generally, and their use of confidential sources in particular, with many reporters borrowing techniques from CIA operatives and members of organized crime to keep information out of the hands of the government, should it come knocking at their doors.

Meanwhile, some traditional news organizations have come under attack for their judgments about what to broadcast or publish. In October 2006, several members of Congress called for the Pentagon to remove embedded CNN reporters from Iraq after the network aired a controversial video showing insurgent snipers targeting American soldiers. Earlier that year the *New York Times* caused a firestorm when it revealed classified information about several secret government programs intended to combat terrorism, eliciting criticism not only from segments of the public, but also from numerous elected officials, some of whom urged criminal prosecution for the disclosure. Although there are laws on the books that arguably would allow charges to be brought for the mere publication of classified information, they never have been employed against a news organization. Some members of Congress are also sponsoring new laws that would criminalize the unauthorized disclosure of classified information. The fact that suggestions these laws should be used against journalists are being taken somewhat seriously is further evidence that news organizations find themselves in troubled times.

Compounding these vexing issues is perhaps an even greater challenge to traditional journalism: the emergence of large numbers of nonprofessionals and nontraditional journalists (including many bloggers) as a significant force in defining and distributing news.

"The center of thinking within journalism is not completely within the newsroom anymore," observes Lew Friedland of the University of Wisconsin-Madison's School of Journalism and Mass Communication. As for "the center of thinking about public life—which is essentially what good journalism is," it is "moving out to hundreds of thousands of people. The Web makes it possible for citizens to think in public together. That is not a fad. That is the underlying reality of the news industry for the next 30 to 50 years."

Many keen media observers acknowledge that a fundamental change in the nature of journalism is at hand. In April 2006, the *Economist* magazine dedicated a substantial part of one of its issues to "new media." Known for its careful analysis, and rarely prone to hyperbole, the *Economist* argued that "society is in the early phases of what appears to be a media revolution on the scale of that launched by Gutenberg [inventor of the printing press] in 1448." The magazine followed that up with an August 2006 cover page and story entitled "Who Killed the Newspaper?" which likewise chronicled fundamental changes facing traditional media organizations. In a recent assessment of the state of journalism, Geneva Overholser (now a professor at the University of Missouri School of Journalism, and formerly editor of the *Des Moines Register*, ombudsman of the *Washington Post*, and member of the *New York Times* editorial board) was more direct: "Journalism as we know it is over."

Journalism schools and professional organizations also seem to be getting the picture. The October 2005 issue of *Quill*, the magazine published by the Society of Professional Journalists, featured an article entitled "Citizen Journalism Continues to Surge." The August 2006 edition of the same magazine included an article warning that "students must prepare for the future of citizen media." Leading journalism publications like the *American Journalism Review* and *Columbia Journalism Review* now regularly discuss journalism by nonprofessionals. And, perhaps even more telling, money is starting to flow to nontraditional journalism ventures from a variety of sources, including foundations, venture capital funds, and wealthy individuals (such as Mark Cuban, the spirited owner of the NBA's Dallas Mavericks as well as several technology and media companies, and Craig Newmark, founder of the wildly successful Web site craigslist).

## How We Got Here:
## The Birth of American Journalism

To fully appreciate the current state of journalism and the transformation underway requires a short review of the origins of American journalism.

The first publications produced at regular intervals appeared in the colonies in the early 1700s, initially in the form of newspapers and later as magazines. These periodicals enjoyed steady growth throughout the eighteenth century, made possible in large part by the government postal system, and in particular by the decision in 1792 to provide financial subsidies for newspapers distributed through the postal system, later extended to magazines as well.

The development of periodicals was also spurred by other factors, like the growth of cities and the spread of public education and literacy (which provided bigger audiences concentrated in smaller areas), as well as by improved and less costly printing. These same forces also gave rise in the 1830s to what is referred to as the "penny press"—a description given to a type of lively, independent daily newspaper sold on street corners for a penny each, considerably less than the more established papers that existed at the time. Supported primarily by advertisers seeking to reach wide audiences, the most popular penny papers sold tens of thousands of copies daily. A number of today's venerable newspapers themselves started as penny papers, including the *New York Times*, the *Chicago Tribune*, and the *Baltimore Sun*.

The arrival of the penny press marked a turning point in American media. Not only did these papers usher in important practices in news coverage—like regularly printing stories about domestic politics—but they heralded a rapid expansion of newspaper readership. By the 1830s, the United States had more than 1,200 newspapers, ninety of which were daily, with newspapers making up 95 percent of the weight of material mailed through the postal system.

The advent of newspaper advertising also marked a turning point in the early history of the American press, allowing publishers a degree of independence from political parties they had not previously enjoyed. During the colonial period the press had been free in the sense that it was unencumbered by obligations to the government, including the absence of taxes like those levied on the press in England. Printers of newspapers, books, and leaflets generally remained agnostic about the viewpoints of their customers, publishing for a price whatever material came their way. But printers needed money, and as more of it came from readers and advertisers, they grew less reliant on political parties themselves.

While the press had largely achieved financial independence from political parties by the mid-1800s, this independence should not be confused with indifference. The press gradually also grew more assertive, taking an increasingly active part in public debate, often with strong political biases of their own. Around the turn of the century, magazines and newspapers began to publish serious investigative pieces. By that point, the daily newspaper had come to dominate the public sphere, and every major city had multiple papers, representing a range of ideological perspectives.

Although the press had developed an independent streak around the 1830s, for much of the next century it was substantially influenced by prevailing political and economic establishments, with reporters rarely exposing the failings of government and leading corporations. In the aftermath of World War I, however, a movement emerged that sought more objectivity and use of evidence by the press. While aspects of what came to be viewed as "journalistic objectivity"—such as detachment, nonpartisanship, an emphasis on facts rather than opinions, balance, and a presentation of "both sides"—had begun to surface decades earlier, adherence to them accelerated after the war. So too did the prevalence of fact-gathering techniques like interviewing, which became widely practiced by 1900, and soon thereafter became a hallmark of American journalism. By the time of World War II, "objectivity" was viewed as the centerpiece of the journalists' code, and became a focal point of journalism education as well as the ethical guidelines of journalism organizations and professional associations.

The emergence of objectivity as journalism's creed occurred in tandem with development of the conception of journalism as a profession. As Michael Schudson, a professor at the University of California, San Diego, explains in *The Sociology of News*, "objectivity seemed a natural and progressive ideology for an aspiring occupational group at a moment when science was God, efficiency was cherished, and increasingly prominent elites judged partisanship a vestige of the tribal nineteenth century." This period featured the creation of several journalism-related professional associations and the development of codes of conduct to guide their budding vocation. For instance, the National Press Club was formed in 1908, and soon thereafter adopted as part of its mission the fostering of "the ethical standards of the profession." The first chapter of what is known today as the Society of Professional Journalists was organized in 1909. And in 1922, newspaper editors started the American Society of Newspaper Editors, the first nationwide professional journalism association.

The country's first journalism schools were also established during this time. The oldest, the Missouri School of Journalism, was founded in 1908 by Walter Williams—who also authored the "Journalist's Creed," an influential ethics code for journalists. Within a decade after the Missouri School of Journalism opened its doors, there were eighty more journalism programs across the country.

Once the view of the press as a profession of objective reporters had taken hold, the idea of the press as a watchdog began to take deeper root. Indeed, as early as the 1950s the press was described as the Fourth Branch of government—reflecting the belief that the press played a critical role in the system of checks and balances characterizing the structure of the federal government. The idea of a press truly adversarial to the government emerged in the McCarthy era, and grew stronger during the Vietnam War and Watergate. The transition from independence to objectivity to a quasi-official adversary of the government was a defining feature of the journalism that emerged during the last century.

## Corporatization of the News Business and Journalism

The latter part of the twentieth century featured another important development for journalism: nearly all significant news organizations were transformed into or acquired by enormous corporations. Most American newspapers were founded by individuals or families. Today, a few large companies control the vast majority of organizations dedicated to the publication of news and related information. And those companies tend to own lots of other businesses, most of which have nothing to do with journalism.

Many news organizations used to be run without regard for the fact that they lost money. This was often acceptable for a number of reasons, including because a company's news division was part of an overall effort to establish the brand of the larger business or, in the case of television and radio, because the news helped fulfill public service requirements imposed on broadcasters by the Federal Communications Commission. But with this more recent wave of consolidation and corporatization has come an increased focus on the profitability of the news businesses enveloped within these companies. This, in turn, has significantly changed the way journalism is practiced.

For example, increased focus on profits has contributed to the proliferation of television news coverage and formats that are inexpensive to produce, like talk shows and other programming based on discussion and opinion, and the virtual disappearance of reports requiring time-consuming newsgathering and investigation. The combination of high ratings and low production costs results in frequent wall-to-wall coverage of celebrity trials, select missing persons cases, and hurricanes and other weather-related events.

When news organizations with limited resources dedicated to newsgathering and analysis actually cover more substantive stories, they tend to end up with a herd mentality, chasing the same ones. And even in those instances, reporting is overwhelmingly composed of regurgitated statements by official sources, or by the reporting of information gathered by another organization—a practice increasingly in vogue. *Washington Post* veterans Len Downie and Robert Kaiser were on the mark when they wrote in their book *The News About the News*, examining the condition of American journalism, that there is often "too little news in the news."

The quest for profits also impels large corporations with news divisions to employ them in promoting or cross-selling their other businesses. Remember that story you recently saw on the local news about the program which happens to run on the same network? How about the piece touting the new CD released by a music label owned by the same company that owns the news station? News seems to have become an extension of these companies' entertainment businesses, as well as a way to promote them. Journalism, it would seem, is fast becoming just another form of content.

Professional journalists are among those complaining loudest about these developments. Downie and Kaiser believe "the drift away from serious coverage of serious subjects was part of the most important change in American news values in the last years of the twentieth century: Covering the news, once seen primarily as a public service that could also make a profit, became primarily a vehicle for attracting audiences and selling advertising, to make money." Bill Kovach and Tom Rosenstiel, chairman and vice chairman of the Committee of Concerned Journalists (a group formed in the late 1990s to undertake a comprehensive examination of journalism and the responsibilities of journalists), have observed in *The Elements of Journalism* that rather than censorship the "new danger is that independent journalism may be dissolved in the solvent of commercial communication and synergistic self-promotion." Reporting on foreign affairs seems to have been particularly hard hit, with Tom Fenton, a correspondent of four decades, remarking that the "mega-corporations that have taken over the major American news companies [have] squeezed the life out of foreign news reporting." The voices of holdouts within large media companies who still believe in grand journalistic ambitions are often drowned out as the role of journalists within these mega-companies diminishes. "The economic imperatives of the communications media, the star system of celebrity journalism and the need to supply the public with constant reinforcement or shock therapy have combined to make fools, not truth-seekers, out of journalists," contends Bruce Sanford, one of the nation's leading media lawyers.

Of course, news organizations do not deserve all the blame for this predicament. While there are many potential explanations for why audience interest in serious news seems to have diminished (including, I suspect, the proliferation of video games and wireless handheld devices that shorten our attention spans), the fact is that most Americans would prefer to be entertained than informed. And it is hard to entirely fault for-profit companies for responding to their customers' interests and desires. Media companies are profit driven, and therefore respond to the actual demands of customers rather than some idealized sense of what they *should* want.

Regardless of who deserves the blame, we are caught in a cycle in which the ambitions of news organizations and the appetites of news consumers are collectively diminishing the breadth and quality of reporting at most news organizations. The public's opinion of the institutional media has been declining for at least two decades, and unhappiness with the media establishment may be a significant cause of what veteran journalist James Fallows aptly describes as a "quiet consumers' boycott of the press." News organizations exacerbate this by themselves melding news with other forms of entertainment. The offerings of news organizations look more and more like just another product vying for the attention of the public—an observation seemingly confirmed by a 2006 study, led by an Indiana University professor, which found coverage of the 2004 presidential election on *The Daily Show with Jon Stewart* substantively comparable with the broadcast television networks' newscasts.

## The "New" Journalism?

More recently injected into this mix are the Internet and the Web. They clearly are not the first important technological innovations to transform journalism. The arrival of the telegraph in the 1830s and 1840s, and later the telephone, introduced powerful news-gathering tools that vastly increased the speed with which information could be transmitted across the country and the world. The commercialization of radio in the 1920s, and television several decades later, gave rise to two important methods of distributing news and other content as a complement (and competitor) to print.

Like prior technological innovations, the Web is a delivery device, not itself content. But what a delivery device it is! In a relatively short time the Web has forced news businesses, as well as other media and communications organizations, to rethink what they do and how they do it.

Why is the Web having such a dramatic effect? Three of its characteristics stand out, and are particularly relevant to its effect on journalism. First, it is inexpensive to access and use. Second, its access and use are unregulated and largely unconstrained by either government rules or physical scarcity. Third, unlike the communications innovations that preceded it, the Web allows the interaction of many-to-many rather than one-to-one (e.g., telegraph and telephone) or one-to-many (e.g., print, television, and radio).

Among other things, the Web has created an enormous supply of people who want to share information and ideas with a wide audience, and there are increasing numbers of people interested in hearing and discussing what they have to say. Many are doing so through "weblogs" (usually shortened to "blogs"), Web-based publications generally consisting of periodic postings and articles (typically arranged in reverse chronological order). Although blogs have been around since about 1992, it was not until 1999, when free software used for blogging became widely available, that their numbers began to increase rapidly.

*Business Week* reported in 2005 that there were nine million blogs, with forty thousand new ones being launched every day. These numbers may have been low at the time, but certainly were out of date a year later. In July 2006, the Web site Technorati, which describes itself as "the recognized authority on what's going on in the world of weblogs," issued a report to commemorate the moment when the number of blogs it tracks exceeded fifty million globally. This reflected a hundred-fold increase in the number of blogs over a three-year period.

Clearly, most bloggers do not aspire to anything other than providing information or entertainment for themselves and a small number of friends and relatives. According to a 2005 survey conducted by America Online, 16 percent of respondents said they blog because they are interested in journalism, while the vast majority do so for other reasons. This sentiment appears to have been corroborated by a 2006 survey conducted by the Pew Internet & American Life Project, which found 34 percent of bloggers consider blogging a form of journalism.

But there are tens of thousands of blogs and Web sites where nontraditional journalists report, analyze, and opine on a range of issues—some covered by their mainstream counterparts, and some not. Many of these efforts are serious and purposeful, and a number of them have gained substantial followings. Several political blogs claim hundreds of thousands of daily viewers.

The growing importance of blogging as a source of news and opinion is evident not just from the number of blogs and their readers. It is also evident from polling conducted during January and February 2007, which found 30 percent of respondents view blogging as an important source of news and information (the figure was above 40 percent for those ages 18–29), while more than 55 percent identify it as important to the future of journalism (65 percent of those ages 18–29).

The growing significance of blogging is also reflected in developments like the founding of the

Media Bloggers Association, "a non-partisan organization dedicated to promoting MBA members and their blogs, educating bloggers, and promoting the explosion of citizen's media," and the formation of many other blogger groups around the country. The MBA, formed in 2004, had over one thousand members in mid-2006, and expects its membership to increase to about ten thousand in the near future. The group received a burst of attention in early 2007 when it obtained two press credentials, to be shared by about a dozen of its members, allowing them special access to the trial of Scooter Libby, and then partnered with the Associated Press for distribution of its members' trial coverage.

But the transformation underway is not limited to blogging. Consider the creation of entities like the Center for Citizen Media, a nonprofit entity affiliated with the University of California, Berkeley, Graduate School of Journalism and the Berkman Center for Internet and Society at Harvard Law School. Formed at the end of 2005, it is an initiative aimed at enabling and encouraging grassroots media and other forms of nontraditional journalism. The center is founded and directed by Dan Gillmor, a former *San Jose Mercury News* columnist and author of *We the Media: Grassroots Journalism by the People, for the People*, published in 2004.

Similar efforts are being undertaken by journalism professors and at a number of journalism schools. Dozens of citizens have taken workshops on reporting basics as part of the Madison Commons, a project led by a journalism professor at the University of Wisconsin-Madison. Another professor, at Ohio University's Scripps School of Journalism, is recruiting and training citizens in three rural villages in southeastern Ohio to create a monthly newsletter and a Web site on local government, schools, business, and organizations, as part of the *Route 7 Report*. The University of South Carolina School of Journalism and Mass Communication has joined with the *Hartsville Messenger*, a twice-weekly publication serving an area of twenty thousand people in that state, to form Hartsville Today, a project to involve citizens in "community storytelling" and "community conversation," envisioned as a pilot to develop insights for other smaller papers that consider "bringing in readers as journalistic collaborators." J-Lab: The Institute for Interactive Journalism, at the University of Maryland's journalism school, has partnered with the Knight Foundation in forming the Knight Citizen News Network, a self-help Web site that seeks to guide "citizens who want to start their own news ventures" and "open the doors to citizen participation for traditional news organizations seeking to embrace user-generated content."

There are several innovative projects underway to

involve citizens in investigation and analysis of Congress. For example, Congresspedia is a not-for-profit, collaborative project of the Center for Media and Democracy and the Sunlight Foundation, developing a "citizen's encyclopedia on Congress." Another project (in which at least one traditional news organization is taking part) will deploy citizens to track and report on the congressional budget process.

Citizen initiatives are not exclusively focused on national issues. A large number of blogs and Web sites led by nonprofessionals concentrate on local issues—often poorly covered by mainstream news organizations. One notable example is a venture called Backfence, which focuses on events and issues in specific towns, providing "opportunities for people to share information with their neighbors and a place for everyone to comment on that information— bringing together the community's collective knowledge." By the end of 2006, Backfence had established Web sites for communities in California, Illinois, Maryland, and Virginia, and planned to move into a dozen more states over the next few years (at least before announcing a management shake-up in January 2007). There are already numerous other "hyperlocal" Web sites set up across the country, with more appearing every week.

Nor are efforts at citizen journalism limited to the Internet. Nonprofessionals are also contributing to television ventures that feature their work. One is Current TV, a cable and satellite channel launched in 2005 by former Vice President Al Gore. Current TV solicits and uses viewer-created submissions, which constitute approximately one-third of its programming content. As of January 2007, it was available in more than 38 million homes in the United States. In late 2006, it entered into a joint venture with Yahoo!, and plans to create a British version to air in Europe. Established television networks are also beginning to get into the act, with several actively soliciting content from their viewers. So, too, is cable giant Comcast, which joined forces with the Web site Facebook.com to create a series from user-generated content that will appear online and through Comcast's video-on-demand service.

Although most established news organizations hate to admit it, nontraditional journalists have become a force in breaking news and analyzing it. Matt Drudge, one of the earliest and most controversial to disseminate political news and commentary through the Internet, broke the story about President Clinton's affair with Monica Lewinsky. His Drudge Report scooped *Newsweek*, which elected not to publish the article it was developing on the Clinton-Lewinsky relationship, and other mainstream journalism powerhouses did not even have the story to publish until after Drudge went with it. The significance of that moment in the history of American journalism is not lost on many professional journalists. Michael Kinsley, who has run the editorial page of the *Los Angeles Times* and edited the *New Republic* magazine as well as the online periodical *Slate*, commented about the Lewinsky scandal: "The Internet made this story. And this story made the Internet. Clintongate, or whatever we are going to call it, is to the Internet what the Kennedy assassination was to TV news: its coming of age as a media force."

Since then, nontraditional journalists have continued shaping the media landscape. For example, in 2002, then–Senate Majority Leader Trent Lott came under fire for praising fellow Senator Strom Thurmond's segregationist campaign for the presidency in 1948, suggesting the nation would have been better off had Thurmond been elected. After an initial wave of criticism, the controversy abated in the mainstream media. However, bloggers continued to hammer on the story, scrutinizing Lott's legislative record on civil rights and past statements about Thurmond's 1948 candidacy, prompting traditional media outlets to pick it up again, ultimately leading to his resignation as majority leader. In 2004, contributors to the conservative blog Power Line were primarily responsible for discrediting documents used in CBS News's unflattering story about President George W. Bush's National Guard service (based in part on expertise about old typewriters), ultimately casting a cloud over Dan Rather and leading to the departure of several others at CBS who worked on the piece. More recently, bloggers uncovered and publicized examples of doctored photographs published by some news organizations during the 2006 conflict between Israel and Hezbollah.

The contributions of citizens working outside established news organizations have not been limited to the disclosure of discrete facts and one-time events. For instance, bloggers—including some active-duty military personnel—have provided important coverage of the conflicts in Iraq and Afghanistan, often supplying information that could not be obtained by mainstream journalists.

There is clearly an interest in the work of these nonprofessionals. More than fifty million Americans turn daily to the Internet for news—a number that is certain to grow. Of those, many look beyond traditional news organizations as sources of information and opinion. One 2006 survey shows that 39 percent of Internet users (57 million American adults) read blogs. According to another, from early 2007, more than 80 percent of respondents view Web sites as an important source of news and information, and most believe blogging and other sources outside of established media are important to the future of journalism.

## The "New" Journalists?

Are these bloggers and other nonprofessionals journalists? Not surprisingly, professional journalists and
the general public tend to see things differently.
According to a study conducted by the University of
Pennsylvania in 2005, 81 percent of professional
journalists resisted the idea that bloggers are journalists. In contrast, an informal poll of readers taken by
the *Christian Science Monitor* in the same year found
that 57 percent of respondents believed bloggers are
journalists and deserve the protections extended to
the press.

I believe the readers have the better view—at least
in the sense that *some* blogging clearly constitutes
journalism. Although the concept of "news" arguably
transcends time and culture, journalism as an idea,
and as a practice, does not. It is only for the past two
or three centuries that people have regularly written
and published true stories about current events. Journalism is a tool for informing one another about the
world's affairs, and helping make sense of it all. Journalists are not a priestly class. They are citizens, just
like the rest of us. In the United States, we are all free
to write down our thoughts and share them with others. Many bloggers and others using the Internet to
distribute ideas and information are engaging in the
same activity as professional journalists (whether they

do it as accurately, or as well, is another matter), and it hardly seems relevant that they use the Web as their method of publication, or that they may not get paid for their efforts.

The century that preceded the emergence of the Web—a period dominated by large news organizations, increasingly controlled by profit-oriented corporations—appears to have hardened an artificial distinction between professional journalists and everyone else. After an extended detour during which the means of mass communication effectively rested in the hands of the few, technological developments, with the Web at its foundation, are unwinding that process and democratizing communications as a whole, and journalism in particular.

In a sense, we are returning to where we started. The institutional press no longer possesses the exclusive means of reaching the public. Anyone can disseminate information to the rest of the world (at least anyone with computer access) at virtually no expense.

So what should we call this new breed of journalism? The list of terms used to describe it is already long and growing: Stand-alone Journalism; Grassroots Journalism; Ad Hoc Journalism; Personal Journalism; Bottom-up Journalism; Participatory Journalism; Networked Journalism; Collaborative Journalism; Open Source Journalism; "We" Journalism; "We-dia" (contrasted with Media); and Citizen Journalism (the term

I generally prefer, and the one I will most often use throughout the book).

All of these terms generally refer to forms of non-traditional journalism, typically practiced by someone who has not (at least heretofore) engaged in journalism to make a living, and who is not associated with what previously might have been viewed as a mainstream media organization. A subset—for instance, Networked or Collaborative Journalism—is, by definition, collective in nature, designed to promote and allow interactive writing and editing. This collective work is largely modeled upon, and inspired by, the success of similar efforts in creating a type of computer software called "open source" that, as the name suggests, allows free access to source code, and permits people to modify and add to the code. This process contributed to the development of the software called Linux, which successfully competes with proprietary software developed by Microsoft and other companies.

Right now traditional media organizations and citizen journalists are circling each other warily, trying to figure out the best way to deal with one another. Although professional journalists tend to have greater resources, citizen journalists have certain advantages of their own. For instance, many bloggers specialize in topics to the extent few professionals employed by media companies can, and the Web arguably provides better error-correction mechanisms than traditional media with large numbers of "fact-checkers" weighing in at warp speed.

While recognizing some of the strengths of bloggers and their Internet brethren, many professional journalists are reluctant to view them as able to make meaningful contributions to journalism. Nicholas Lemann, dean of Columbia University's Graduate School of Journalism, drew considerable criticism from bloggers for his 2006 article in the *New Yorker*, provocatively entitled "Amateur Hour," which examined the role of nonprofessional journalists, and concluded that, as of now, "there is not much relation between claims for the possibilities inherent in journalist-free journalism and what people engaged in that pursuit are actually producing." Another Columbia professor, Samuel Freedman, was more blunt, recoiling at the notion of calling nonprofessionals "journalists," and claiming that the citizen journalism movement "forms part of a larger attempt to degrade, even to disenfranchise, journalism as practiced by trained professionals."

Similar skepticism about the virtues of journalism performed by nonprofessionals has been expressed by Fred Brown, a past president of the century-old Society of Professional Journalists, the largest of the nation's journalism associations, who wrote a "traditional journalist's" responsibility is to find and report "new and accurate information," while blogs are "good at finding flaws in others' information" and the priority of a nontraditional journalist is "to be interesting." *USA Today* columnist Andrew Kantor similarly chided "amateur" journalists for their penchant to "make up the rules as they go" and "blow small things out of proportion."

Some media observers critique bloggers and other nonprofessionals on the grounds they have a parasitic relationship with mainstream news organizations. As Richard Posner, the prolific author and federal judge, wrote in the *New York Times Book Review*, "the legitimate gripe of the conventional media is not that bloggers undermine the overall accuracy of news reporting, but that they are free riders who may in the long run undermine the ability of the conventional media to finance the very reporting on which bloggers depend."

Others decry nonprofessional journalists because they muddy the waters at a time when we need professional journalists more than ever, to filter and interpret the wealth of information available in the Internet age. Today, they claim, the press's sorting, selecting, and judging functions are more important than ever.

In the midst of this criticism, part of the response of the mainstream media to the phenomenon is to co-opt or imitate it, explicitly recognizing the existence of citizen journalists and seeking to bring them into the fold in limited respects. MSNBC, for instance, set up a section of its Web site for "citizen journalists," from which it doles out "assignments" to these intrepid volunteers, and then posts some of their reports. CBS News revamped its Web site to add a blog for commentary about its work, and CNN solicits viewer video and commentary on its Web site. Gannett, the nation's largest newspaper chain and owner of *USA Today*, announced in November 2006 that it was substantially restructuring its business, in part to integrate elements of citizen journalism. In February 2007, the Associated Press announced it had teamed up with NowPublic.com, a Vancouver-based participatory news network with 60,000 contributors from 140 countries, to incorporate citizen contributions into Associated Press reporting. Other traditional news organizations are employing similar strategies.

Regardless of how the relationship between mainstream media and citizen journalists unfolds, it is clear that online and other nontraditional journalists will play an increasingly significant role in American life. And this has, and will, engender resistance from some. History teaches us that when older news media are confronted by newer ones, debates over the nature of news and journalism often ensue. We are witnessing the beginning of such debates.

Consider *Apple Computer v. Doe 1*. This controversy—a David versus Goliath story with a dash of corporate espionage mixed in—is among the first of what will be many Internet-era legal disputes wrestling with the question: "Who is a journalist?"

The drama kicked off in December 2004 when technology juggernaut Apple Computer (maker of Mac computers and iPods, among other devices) filed a lawsuit in a California state court against unnamed individuals (identified in court papers as "Does," like Jane Doe or Jim Doe) who allegedly leaked information about new technologies being developed by Apple to several Web sites that focus on the company and its products, including AppleInsider and Power-Page. Apple claimed that these unnamed Does, who had given information to the Web sites, unlawfully disclosed the company's "trade secrets," and sought damages from the alleged perpetrators.

Apple could not proceed with its case, however, without figuring out the names of the unidentified "Does" who it believed had shared its trade secrets, now broadcast to the public through the Web. One of Apple's first steps after filing its lawsuit was to seek documents from a company called nfox, the e-mail service provider for PowerPage, one of the Web sites that published information about Apple's new technology and unreleased products, which could reveal the identity of the person(s) who disclosed the information to PowerPage.

PowerPage, and other Web sites from whom

Apple sought similar information, asked the court to block Apple's efforts to obtain documents that would reveal how and from whom they had obtained information about Apple's unreleased products. Part of their argument to the court was that as journalists they are protected from such inquiries by California and federal law.

The trial court judge in the case, after noting that figuring out who is a "journalist" has "become more complicated as the variety of media has expanded," avoided deciding whether the sponsors of these Web sites are journalists, ruling that even if they are, Apple was entitled to the information it sought regarding the identity of the "Does" who supposedly disclosed its trade secrets.

The sponsors of the Web sites appealed that decision contending, as they did before the trial court judge, that as "journalists" they are entitled to protection from Apple's efforts to obtain the identity of their sources. In support of their argument they submitted testimony from Dan Gillmor, author of *We the Media*, in which he expressed his view that the Web sites at issue are "news periodicals" like newspapers and magazines, and that the publishers, editors, and authors connected with those Web sites "are engaged in the process of journalism, disseminating information to the public that they have sought, gathered, received or processed with that intent."

Apple, for its part, disputed that the Web site sponsors are journalists or that they are entitled to shield their sources on the basis of California law or the First Amendment of the United States Constitution.

In a widely anticipated ruling, the California Court of Appeals decided in favor of the Web sites and against Apple. Specifically, the court rejected Apple's argument that the online publications could not rely on the protections of California's statute shielding journalists from certain information requests because they were not engaged in "legitimate" journalism. As the court explained:

> We decline the implicit invitation to embroil ourselves in questions of what constitutes "legitimate journalis[m]." The shield law is intended to protect the gathering and dissemination of *news*, and that is what petitioners did here. We can think of no workable test or principle that would distinguish "legitimate" from "illegitimate" news. Any attempt by courts to draw such a distinction would imperil a fundamental purpose of the First Amendment, which is to identify the best, most important, and most valuable ideas not by any sociological or economic formula, rule of law, or process of government, but through the rough and tumble competition of the . . . marketplace.

The opinion went on to emphasize that "courts must be extremely wary about deciding what information is worthy of publication and what information is not," and keenly observed that the "decentralization of expressive capacity" made possible by technological developments "is unquestionably one of the most significant cultural developments since the invention of the printing press."

Faced with a resounding rejection of its arguments, Apple surprised many observers when it announced that it was abandoning its effort to compel the disclosure of the leakers, and did not appeal the ruling.

The *Apple* case is just one of what will be many skirmishes in the years to come forcing us to consider what journalism is in the Internet age, and how non-traditional journalists should be treated relative to professional journalists and members of the institutional media.

Some of these struggles will be waged quietly, outside the limelight—such as that of one blogger, whose request for press credentials to cover the Kentucky General Assembly was denied by the state, or another whose request for media credentials to cover a state transportation conference was rejected by the Texas Department of Transportation and who was told the department was accepting applications only from "mainstream news media."

Others will garner more attention, as with the case of Josh Wolf, a self-described independent journalist and filmmaker, who operates his own Web site, The Revolution Will Be Televised. Wolf was jailed in August 2006 for failing to comply with a federal court order requiring that he turn over his video recording of a June 2005 riot between anarchists and the San Francisco police, sought as part of an investigation of damage to a city police car.

The trial court judge who ordered Wolf to produce his video recording accepted his argument that he was a journalist, as the term is used in California's "shield law" protecting journalists from such requests under limited circumstances. The judge, nevertheless, concluded that California law did not authorize Wolf's refusal in this case. A court of appeals agreed, rejecting Wolf's arguments. Wolf spent a total of 226 days in prison before his release in early April 2007, when he apparently was finally able to convince prosecutors he did not have information important to their investigation. Wolf had been imprisoned longer than any other American journalist.

Wolf's saga is noteworthy not just for the length of his incarceration. Typically, efforts to coerce the disclosure of information and material used for newsgathering trigger briefs from a host of major media organizations in support of the journalist resisting such efforts. In Wolf's case, several journalism interest groups and professional associations filed briefs on his behalf, and the Society of Professional Journalists contributed over $30,000 toward his legal defense, but no organizations that themselves practice journalism elected to do so, despite having filed briefs in support of traditional journalists in other cases, including those called before the grand jury investigating the Plame matter.

The reluctance of mainstream media organizations to recognize nontraditional and citizen journalists as "journalists" is evident in other areas—and will play a significant role in the effort by a new and growing generation of nonprofessionals to avoid being relegated to second-class status.

The media establishment's claim of priority over other citizens is pervasive—and accepted at many levels of federal and state government. Whatever the merits of this perspective in the past, the transformation of journalism necessitates that we reconsider the practice of reflexively extending professional journalists rights and privileges not available to others engaged in the practice of journalism.

There is no doubt that we are all well served by having a cadre of energetic, smart, and well-funded professional journalists on the lookout for the rest of us—and there would be cause for alarm if they disappeared. But the reality is that professional journalists do not go most places, or see most things. Much of what is worth knowing, and worth thinking about, is neglected by the mainstream media. Now, with the rise of citizen journalism, many more people are passing on their observations and ideas, playing a role previously occupied only by members of the institutional press. Journalism has been elegantly described as carrying on and amplifying conversation among the people themselves. The Web and other technological advances have enabled many more of us to participate in these conversations.

Who is a journalist? Should journalists be given rights and privileges not enjoyed by other citizens? It is time for us to confront these questions directly and thoughtfully. We all have a stake in how they are answered.

# CHAPTER TWO

# The Press and the Public Under the Constitution

---

Notwithstanding the recent unpopularity of traditional news organizations and professional journalists with much of the public, most Americans instinctively recognize the importance of a "free press." But what is the basis for our conviction that "the press" must remain "free"—whatever these terms mean?

The fact that the First Amendment specifically guarantees freedom of the press does *not* appear to be the basis for our outlook. In fact, remarkably few people appear to know the First Amendment contains a provision discussing freedom of the press. According to an annual survey conducted since 1997, no more than 16 percent of respondents have identified "freedom of the press" as a right guaranteed by the First Amendment (the figure was down to 13 percent in the 2006 survey). Instead, our commitments to the values associated with a "free press" appear to derive from long-standing and enduring ideas about the role of the press in our lives, and its contribution to our system of government.

One image of the press focuses on its role alerting and informing the public about issues of importance. James Madison believed that "a popular Government without popular information, or the means of acquiring it, is but a prologue to a farce or a tragedy or perhaps both." To Madison and other Founders, the press played an indispensable role in facilitating informed public discussion, itself necessary for properly functioning government and for the preservation of democracy. This view—sometimes called the "structural model" of the press—remains widely held today, and is often invoked by those defending controversial press activities.

A second image of the press (one closely related to the structural model) describes it as a "watchdog," acting as an agent or surrogate for the general public—

protecting the interests of less-attentive or under-informed citizens by adopting skeptical and often adversarial positions vis-à-vis government or other large and powerful institutions.

Of all the press's functions in American life, to many its watchdog role is the most crucial. In fact, the potential of the press as a check against government power and corruption is so considerable that the press is frequently likened to a branch of government—first dubbed the Fourth Branch (along with the executive, legislative, and judicial branches of the federal government) in 1959, by author Douglass Cater. Under this view, the press serves a quasi-official function in our political system, and in many respects is elevated to "the highest rung on society's organizational chart," in the words of First Amendment scholar and Columbia University president Lee Bollinger.

It should be no surprise that the watchdog image of the press remains popular with today's professional journalists. Legendary White House reporter Helen Thomas published a book in 2006 entitled *Watchdogs of Democracy?: The Waning Washington Press Corps and How It Has Failed the Public*, in which she excoriated many of her colleagues for failing to fulfill their watchdog duties. Numerous other books and articles by journalists and journalism observers make clear that the watchdog self-image is alive and well.

A third image of the press's role in society is sometimes described as the "speech model." In the words of the late Supreme Court Justice William Brennan, under this view "the primary purpose of the First Amendment is more or less absolutely to prohibit any interference with freedom of expression," and the press is often conceived of as "simply a collection of individuals who wish to speak out and broadly disseminate their views."

Also sometimes referred to as the "open press model," this outlook is rooted in the conviction that individuals have a right to disseminate their viewpoints for all to consider, and a right to hear a variety of voices. Freedom of the press, from this perspective, represents and promotes the rights of nonpress citizens to speak and to benefit from information and ideas provided by others. To some adherents of this view, freedom of expression is not simply an end unto itself, but the engine for a "marketplace of ideas," which provides the best chance for uncovering truth.

These perspectives about the virtues of a free press have played an important role in shaping government policy toward traditional news organizations, and contributed significantly to a system in which professional journalists are granted rights and privileges not available to other citizens—to be discussed in detail in Chapter 3. Yet, generally speaking, those perks are not extended based on the belief that the *Constitution itself* confers or requires them. Instead, they typically depend on the views of legislators, regulators, civil servants, and in some instances judges, that bestowing such preferences is a good idea.

Before we survey and examine this broad array of press preferences, however, we must understand what our Constitution says about a free press, and how the courts—particularly the United States Supreme Court—have interpreted the Constitution when asked to define "the press" and the nature of press freedom.

## The Meaning of the "Press Clause" of the First Amendment

Four years after adoption of the Constitution in 1787, the Founders set out to fill some of the voids in the nation's foundational legal document by adding ten amendments, collectively known as the Bill of Rights. The first of these amendments forbade Congress from making any law abridging "freedom . . . of the press."

Just what does the Press Clause of the First Amendment mean? What is the nature of the freedom it guarantees?

Judges and lawyers typically begin any interpretive task by examining the language at issue—in this case, the words of the First Amendment and the Press Clause in particular. Here, the text itself is of little help. The First Amendment does not identify who or what qualifies as "the press," nor does it describe the character of the "freedom" for the press that it prescribes.

In addition to the words themselves, the history underlying the enactment of a constitutional provision is frequently consulted as part of the interpretive process. Here too, however, we are left with minimal guidance at best.

The terms "freedom of speech" and "freedom of the press" were often used interchangeably during the eighteenth century, and the meaning of the Speech and Press Clauses of the First Amendment was not evident at the time of their adoption. Although Congress debated the First Amendment's provisions regarding religion, there was virtually no discussion of the language related to freedom of speech or of the press. The state legislatures that ratified the First Amendment likewise offered little that might inform us about their understanding of the provisions related to speech and the press.

There is also considerable debate among historians and legal scholars about whether, and to what extent, the First Amendment's Speech and Press Clauses were intended to institute broad reform of the then prevailing approach to freedom of expression. Skeptics about the claim that reform was the Founders' aim point to the Sedition Act of 1798, passed only seven years after adoption of the First Amendment, which criminalized "any false, scandalous or malicious writing or writings against the government of the United States" with "the intent to defame . . . or to bring them . . . into contempt or disrepute." Although enactment of the Sedition Act was met with hostility from many quarters, and is described by some as the first constitutional crisis after ratification of the Constitution, the fact that many individuals involved in the adoption of the First Amendment saw fit to enact a law banning criticism of the government deepens uncertainty about the Founders' conceptions of the "freedoms" protected by the amendment. And whatever they may have meant by "press freedom," the Founders apparently had no reluctance in excluding the press from the Constitutional Convention itself, and barring delegates from discussing the proceedings.

One of the few unmistakable objectives of enacting the First Amendment, however, was to prohibit the conditioning of written expression on the securing of a license from the government. Although the idea that a license would be required to publish is hard to imagine now, the practice was prevalent in England, and carried across the ocean to some of the British colonies, where a licensing system was in place until the end of the seventeenth century. Historians and scholars agree that the prevention of that restraint was a leading purpose in the adoption of the Press Clause.

Another thing clear about the First Amendment is that, when written, journalism as we know it today did not exist. The press in the eighteenth century was a trade of printers, and "those who called for 'freedom of the press' in the seventeenth and eighteenth centuries had in mind books and pamphlets and all kinds of occasional literature as much as newspapers," notes Anthony Lewis, the longtime *New York Times* reporter who won a Pulitzer Prize for his coverage of the Supreme Court and has written extensively about the First Amendment.

Beyond these few insights, it is not at all clear to me what those involved in the adoption of the First Amendment intended when they included the Press Clause. I am not alone. Most who have considered what the drafters of the First Amendment sought to accomplish by adding the four words of the Press Clause to the amendment find the evidence inconclusive.

## The Supreme Court and "Press" Rights

While the history leading to adoption of the First Amendment does not tell us much, given the prominent placement in the Constitution of the language about press freedom and the important functions performed by "the press," one might expect the Supreme Court to have seized upon the specific reference to freedom of "the press" in the First Amendment as a basis for defining the press and explaining the nature of press freedoms. Quite the opposite has happened. The Press Clause has played almost no role in constitutional law, and its meaning remains something of a mystery. How could this be?

As an initial matter, the Court was slow in even addressing cases involving the Press Clause. Although the First Amendment was added to the Constitution in 1791 (along with the other nine of the first ten amendments, composing the Bill of Rights), Supreme Court cases rarely dealt with free speech or press issues before the 1900s. In fact, in 1951, the Court itself asserted that it had not decided any "important" cases involving free speech until 1919. While this is almost certainly an overstatement, it is clear the Court did not begin to robustly *defend* free speech or press rights until several decades into the twentieth century.

Why did it take nearly 150 years before the Court began in earnest giving content to the words in the First Amendment addressing freedom of expression and developing the rights we take for granted today?

Part of the answer is provided by examining the interrelationship between the development of legal doctrines on the one hand and prevailing societal views and external events on the other. Prior to World War I, the judiciary in general was unwelcoming of free speech claims, and the justices on the United States Supreme Court were no exception. Although sentiment for broader rights to free expression was spreading before the war, repression of speech and dissent during and after the conflict made many Americans sensitive for the first time to infringements of free expression. The end of the war coincided with the emergence of the modern civil liberties movement in the United States, which facilitated a judicial transformation of the First Amendment over the subsequent decades.

Another part of the answer relates to a somewhat technical, but important, legal rule having to do with the scope of the First Amendment's proscriptions and their relationship to other parts of the Constitution. The precise words of the First Amendment limit only the actions of *Congress* ("Congress shall make no law . . ."); they do *not* apply to other federal government actors, or to the states or their officials. Therefore, based only on the words themselves, the First Amendment does nothing to forbid a governor, town mayor, or local sheriff from impinging freedom of speech or of the press. Although that view of the amendment's scope prevailed for more than a century after the Constitution was adopted, it was eventually abandoned, in part based on a subsequent constitutional amendment.

Ratified in 1868, the Fourteenth Amendment to the federal Constitution provides that no state shall "deprive any person of life, liberty, or property, without due process of law; nor deny to any person within its jurisdiction the equal protection of the laws." About sixty years after enactment of the amendment— in what proved to be a turning point in American legal history—the Supreme Court concluded that most of the provisions of the Bill of Rights also apply to the states and to local governments because these rights had been *incorporated* into the Fourteenth Amendment's guarantees of "due process" and "equal protection." This came to be known as the "incorporation doctrine."

Since most of the cases making their way to the Supreme Court dealt with conduct occurring at the state and local level, rather than with action by Congress, the birth of the incorporation doctrine gave the Court a steady diet of cases where parties claimed they had been denied rights guaranteed by the First Amendment. This enabled the Court to gradually but steadily develop the framework of rules regarding freedom of expression in which we now operate.

While the Court has developed a voluminous body of First Amendment law regarding freedom of expression during the course of the last century, it largely has continued to ignore the Press Clause itself. Several cases decided during the mid-1900s contained terse references to press freedom and distinguished it from freedom of speech. In recent years, the Court has moved even further away from the Press Clause, tending to favor the use of more general terms, such as "speech and press freedom" and "freedom of expression," when addressing arguments raised by news organizations or presented with questions about the scope and nature of press rights.

More important than its use of terminology is the fact that the Supreme Court has *never* determined the Press Clause has any meaning or significance distinct from the Speech Clause of the First Amendment. In its many decisions involving the media and news organizations, the Court has based its rulings on free speech rights that *belong to the press equally with others*. In so doing, the Court has declined requests to exempt journalists from laws and rules that apply to other citizens. The Court has also stated on many occasions where news organizations have asserted special rights of access to places and information that *members of the press have no more rights to such access than other citizens*. As a result, the constitutional protections most important to press freedom are based on the Speech Clause of the First Amendment and apply to all speakers. Whatever freedom the press enjoys has little, if anything, to do with the Press Clause itself. By interpreting the First Amendment's Speech Clause broadly enough to include whatever right was being asserted by the press in a particular case, the Supreme Court has avoided deciding whether there are *any* circumstances under which "the press" has rights or privileges under the Constitution not available to others.

There was a point, however, when it appeared the Court might move in another direction. One of the most forceful arguments that the Press Clause confers special rights on the press not enjoyed by others was advanced more than three decades ago by Supreme Court Justice Potter Stewart—who is perhaps best known to many for saying about pornographic obscenity that, while hard to define, "I know it when I see it." But Stewart's argument did not come in a Court decision. It was set out in a now famous 1974 address at Yale Law School. In that speech, Stewart argued not only that the Press Clause of the First Amendment protects rights different from the Speech Clause, but that the Press Clause "extends protection to an *institution*"—namely institutional or traditional news organizations (what he also referred to as the "organized press"). Under his reading of the First Amendment, the "publishing business" is "the only organized private business that is given explicit constitutional protection." He believed "the press" was afforded this preferred status in order "to create a fourth institution outside the Government as an additional check on the three official branches" of the federal government.

Yet in the years following Stewart's address, the Supreme Court has never come close to adopting the view of the Press Clause and institutional press rights espoused in his speech at Yale. In fact, Stewart never went quite as far in his own opinions written as a member of the Court as he did in his speech, although he clearly was a strong proponent of shielding the institutional media from searches and compelled disclosures of information that might chill their activities.

Nor was Stewart's view consistent with how the Court had described the nature of press freedom prescribed in the First Amendment in the limited number of cases where it had addressed the issue prior to Stewart's remarks. Rather than conceive of "press" rights as belonging to an *institution* (or its members), as far back as the 1920s and 1930s, the Court repeatedly described freedom of the press as a "personal" right.

For example, in 1938, the Court was asked to consider the challenge by a Jehovah's Witness to a Georgia local ordinance that prohibited distribution of "circulars, handbooks, advertising or literature of any kind" without permission from the city manager. After noting that freedom of speech and freedom of the press are both "fundamental *personal* rights and liberties," the Court invalidated the law, which it found "strikes at the very foundation of the freedom of the press by subjecting it to license and censorship." It also noted that press freedoms are not limited to newspapers and periodicals, but extend to pamphlets and leaflets of the sort distributed in the case before the Court. "The press in its historic connotation comprehends every sort of publication which affords a vehicle of information and opinion," the Court explained.

In the ensuing decades the Court continued to characterize the press freedom of the First Amendment as a personal right, and one not confined to the modes of expression employed by large media organizations. In deciding a libel case in 1967, the Court described "the freedom of speech and press" as a "guarantee to individuals of their personal right to make their thoughts public and put them before the community."

It was in 1972, two years before Stewart's speech, however, that the Supreme Court decided one of its most important cases involving the press—one that continues to cause mischief to this day. *Branzburg v. Hayes* involved claims by several employees of traditional news organizations that the First Amendment immunized them from having to respond to subpoenas requiring them to provide to grand juries information they obtained as part of their newsgathering efforts and used for their stories or reports.

By a 5–4 vote, the Supreme Court rejected the reporters' contentions that they should be exempt from compliance with the subpoenas. Three of the Court's nine members joined an opinion by Justice Byron White, in which he wrote that the First Amendment "does not invalidate every incidental burdening of the press that may result from the enforcement of civil or criminal statutes of general applicability," and "does not guarantee the press a constitutional right of special access to information not available to the public generally." In light of their view of the First Amendment, the four justices declined to interpret it as granting "newsmen a testimonial privilege that other citizens do not enjoy."

A fifth Court member, Lewis Powell, agreed with his four colleagues regarding the result of the case as it related to the specific parties before the Court, but wrote separately to "add" his own "statement" emphasizing the "limited nature" of the Court's decision, stating "the Court does *not* hold that newsmen, subpoenaed to testify before a grand jury, are without constitutional rights with respect to gathering of news or in safeguarding their sources." Instead, he suggested a case-by-case determination of a claim to a First Amendment privilege for "newsmen," to be "judged on its facts by the striking of proper bal-

ance between freedom of the press and the obligation of all citizens to give relevant testimony with
respect to criminal conduct." He also wrote that,
contrary to the assertions of the four dissenting
members of the Court, the majority had not determined that "state and federal authorities are free to
'annex' the news media as 'an investigative arm of
government,'" and that "no harassment of newsmen
will be tolerated."

Because Justice Powell cast the deciding vote in
*Branzburg* for an otherwise equally divided Court,
his opinion has become a focus of attention for those
trying to interpret and apply the decision in the
decades ever since. Unfortunately, the debate over the
meaning of Powell's decision, and therefore of
*Branzburg* itself, has bordered on chaos.

As a threshold matter, there is disagreement
about whether Justice Powell joined the opinion of
Justice White and three others (which would make
Justice White's opinion one rendered by a majority
of the Court) and simply *added* separate remarks, or
whether the decision was effectively a 4–1–4, without any majority opinion (which would make Justice
White's remarks what is called a "plurality" opinion). The distinction is important, since majority
decisions carry considerably more weight than ones
decided by only a plurality of the justices.

At the time *Branzburg* was decided, in an opinion

written by Justice Stewart, three of the dissenting justices described Powell's concurrence as "enigmatic." As the years have passed, the enigmatic quality of *Branzburg* has only intensified. Thus, in a 2005 submission to the Court seeking review of the lower court's adverse ruling in the Plame case, lawyers for *Time* magazine's parent company accurately advised the Court: "the confusion generated by Justice Powell's concurrence has persisted for more than three decades now, and shows no signs of abating, as courts cannot agree on Justice Powell's exact position, and how (if at all) it modifies Justice White's opinion for the Court."

Even without the uncertainty generated by Powell's concurring opinion, the opinion of Justice White itself left open many issues. This is largely the result of how judge-made law develops. Courts render decisions based on the facts presented in specific cases before them. Sometimes judges are clear that their decision is not meant to apply to future cases, and should be narrowly read by lawyers and other judges. Other times, judges set out to announce more general rules, to be applied beyond the circumstances of the case in front of them. Yet even in those circumstances, courts cannot anticipate every question that might arise— and generally do not even try to do so. Therefore, like many Court decisions, *Branzburg* gave rise to more questions than it answered.

In *Branzburg*, according to the majority of the justices, "the sole issue" before them was "the obligation of reporters to respond to grand jury subpoenas as other citizens do and to answer questions relevant to any investigation into the commission of a crime." The Court answered that question. However, it provided little guidance about many other related issues. What about efforts to seek information from reporters for use at stages in a criminal case other than a grand jury proceeding? Does the First Amendment provide any protection for "newsmen" when information is sought from them for use in a civil case—where the stakes for the parties are lower than they are in a criminal case?

These are precisely the kinds of questions that have been presented to the Supreme Court in the more than three decades since *Branzburg*. Despite frequent requests to revisit that ruling and address these issues, the Court has declined to do so.

The Court has, nevertheless, addressed numerous cases concerning news organizations in the years since *Branzburg*. In the intervening decades, the Court has considered, and invariably rejected, arguments by established news organizations that because they are members of "the press" they should be exempt from laws that apply to others. During this period, the Court has also repeated several times its view that the Constitution does not confer on "the press" any right of access to information greater than the right of the general public.

In its rhetoric, the Court has consistently described the vital role of the institutional press in society. On various occasions it has praised the press for advancing our democratic system—seemingly adhering to the structural model of the press discussed above. Several times, for instance, it has observed that "informed public opinion is the most potent of all restraints upon misgovernment," and it has called a "free press" one of the "great interpreters between the government and the people."

The Court has also repeatedly embraced the watchdog conception of the press—several times using the term itself. In a 1965 ruling addressing the propriety of televising a high-profile criminal trial, the Court observed that the "free press has been a mighty catalyst" for "exposing corruption among officers and employees." A year later, in striking down an Alabama statute that made it a crime for a newspaper to publish an editorial on election day urging people to vote a particular way, the Court wrote "the press serves and was designed to serve as a powerful antidote to any abuses of power by governmental officials and as a constitutionally chosen means for keeping officials elected by the people responsible to all the people whom they were selected to serve." A 1983 decision, invalidating a Minnesota "use tax" on the consumption of paper and ink products used for the production of publications, described the notion that "the press will often serve as an important restraint on government" as "the basic assumption of our political system."

Notwithstanding its praise for the contributions of the institutional press, the Supreme Court has never been willing to move beyond mere recognition of the press's importance, and rule that any provision in the Constitution *requires* either exempting "the press" from generally applicable laws (i.e., laws to apply to everyone) or extending to "the press" any special privileges (such as rights of access not available to the general public). The Court's approach is exemplified by a 1978 decision, striking down a Massachusetts criminal statute prohibiting businesses from making contributions to influence the outcome of voter referendum proposals. Referring to the press as an institution, the Court acknowledged its "special and constitutionally recognized role . . . in informing and educating the public, offering criticism, and providing a forum for discussion and debate." Nevertheless, the Court dismissed arguments that the institutional press should have a preferred status under the Constitution, observing that it "does not have a monopoly" on the First Amendment "or on the ability to enlighten."

## First Amendment "Press" Rights
## in the Lower Federal Courts

Although the Supreme Court has decided numerous cases involving news organizations and journalists since *Branzburg*, it has managed to do so without either directly revisiting that decision or squarely addressing the meaning of the Press Clause and whether it entitles "the press" to preferential treatment.

As a general matter, the United States Supreme Court is the ultimate arbiter of meaning of the federal Constitution. Because of the Court's reluctance to expound upon its ruling in *Branzburg*, lower federal courts and state courts interpreting and applying the provisions of the Constitution have been left to their own devices about these issues, and they (along with legal scholars) have formed wildly divergent views about the reach of the decision, and whether it leaves any room for interpreting the First Amendment as providing protections to "the press" that are not available to others.

It did not take long after *Branzburg* was decided for these fissures to form, and for the process of limiting the opinion to begin. Many courts determined that with the decision the Supreme Court had not intended to reject altogether the claim of a First Amendment privilege for the press, except on the specific facts of that case. It took only a matter of months for one court to reach the conclusion that, notwithstanding *Branzburg*, journalists are entitled to some form of immunity under the First Amendment when information is sought from them. Within a mere five years after *Branzburg*, one of the federal courts of appeals proclaimed that the existence of some First Amendment privilege is "no longer in doubt."

One of the Court's justices, William Brennan, seemingly contributed to uncertainty about the scope of the *Branzburg* decision when, in 1980, he decided a matter before him but not the Court as a whole, and wrote: "I do not believe that the Court has foreclosed news reporters from resisting a subpoena on First Amendment grounds."

Thus, over time, a majority of the federal courts of appeals have recognized some form of "press privilege" under the First Amendment. Yet these courts hold differing views about the scope of such a privilege, including to whom it might pertain. They also disagree about when such a privilege applies. Some have found that the First Amendment privilege is available in both civil and criminal cases. Others have concluded that it applies in civil cases, but not criminal cases.

But at least two courts of appeals have not found there is a First Amendment privilege in *either* civil or criminal cases—one has rejected the idea, and the other has yet to express a view. In 2003, the court that has not taken a firm position accused judges on other courts of "essentially ignor[ing] *Branzburg*," asserting some "audaciously declare that *Branzburg* actually created a reporter's privilege," and fittingly observing that the approaches some have taken to the issue of a First Amendment press privilege "can certainly be questioned."

More than three decades after *Branzburg*, few would dispute that the law in this area is in disarray. It is difficult to think of a modern Supreme Court case addressing an undeniably important issue that has generated such divergent views among the lower courts, over such a long period of time, without intervening guidance from the high court. Nevertheless, the Supreme Court has elected to stand on the sidelines.

One of the recent efforts to get the Court to bring order to the chaos was the request for review filed by *Time* and the *New York Times* from an unfavorable ruling requiring them to disclose information sought by the government in the Plame investigation. In their petition to the Court the lawyers for *Time* appropriately told the justices that "whatever the intended meaning of *Branzburg*, the lower courts have been interpreting the decision, and Justice Powell's concurrence, in radically, intolerably different ways, resulting in a patchwork of inconsistent and conflicting legal standards." The Court declined the request for review, as it has done repeatedly since rendering the *Branzburg* decision in 1972.

## The Future of the Press Clause and of Claims to Preferences Under the First Amendment

What does the future hold for the Press Clause, and for efforts to convince the Supreme Court that the provision entitles the press to special rights and privileges? Will the Supreme Court continue to treat the Press Clause as largely an extension of the Speech Clause, with the institutional press treated as simply another speaker? Or might we expect a change of course, with the Court finally vesting the Press Clause with meaning and significance separate and apart from the First Amendment's Speech Clause? Will the Court continue to view press freedom as a personal right, or come to the view that institutions or organizations engaged in press activities do enjoy some constitutional rights beyond those enjoyed by other citizens?

Although we know the Court has declined a number of requests in recent years to take up cases that would have allowed it to reach these issues, the process at the Court for deciding whether to hear cases is carried out behind closed doors, and except in rare instances the public is provided no information about why the Court declined to hear a matter, or how many justices might have been in favor of taking up a given issue. We therefore have no way of knowing whether any members of the Court share the view of lawyers, commentators, and lower court judges that there is a need for the Supreme Court to revisit *Branzburg* and weigh in on questions related to freedom of the press.

In the view of some Court watchers, the justices have gone out of their way in recent decades to avoid addressing the Press Clause and the question whether it has any meaning apart from the Speech Clause. The Court's repeated denial of requests for review on these issues certainly provides good reason to think the Court will continue to evade hard questions concerning the nature of press freedom and the meaning of the Press Clause.

At the same time, there are several reasons to think the Court may revisit *Branzburg* and its attendant exploration of the nature of press freedom, or otherwise embark on a reexamination of the Press Clause.

First, the Court's current interpretation of the First Amendment effectively reads it as if the Press Clause were not there. This view of the amendment is hard to reconcile with an approach to constitutional interpretation that focuses on the plain language of a provision, which is favored by some current Court members. It is also at odds with a fundamental tenet of constitutional interpretation that no word was unnecessarily used in, or needlessly added to, the document. Justices who consider the views of the Founders as a principal source of guidance in interpreting the Constitution may also look skeptically at the prevailing view of the Press Clause, since it would have been unnecessary to include it in the First Amendment were it simply redundant of the amendment's free speech guarantee.

Second, the Court will be provided in the coming years with ample opportunities to revisit the Press Clause and to reassess the nature of press freedom, should it choose to do so. The escalation of efforts to force journalists to reveal their sources is, by itself, likely to present the Court with a steady number of such cases. So too should lawsuits challenging prevailing ideas of who qualifies as a "journalist," which are sure to increase in the decade ahead (discussed more in Chapter 4).

One recent case that seemed like a plausible candidate for high court review concerned two *San Francisco Chronicle* reporters sentenced to as long as 18 months in jail for failing to reveal information to prosecutors investigating alleged steroid use by athletes, possibly including baseball all-star Barry Bonds.

Mark Fainaru-Wada and Lance Williams published a series of articles in the *Chronicle*, and later authored a book, *Game of Shadows*, examining the alleged distribution of steroids and other performance-enhancing drugs to a number of prominent athletes by the Bay Area Laboratory Co-Operative (BALCO). As part of their reporting, Fainaru-Wada and Williams quoted secret testimony given to the grand jury examining BALCO. Prosecutors investigating the leaked testimony issued subpoenas to Fainaru-Wada and Williams, requiring them to appear before the grand jury and produce documents regarding their sources. They refused, and were held in contempt by a federal judge, who rejected their arguments that either the First Amendment or federal "common law" entitled them to resist the subpoena. Prosecutors, however, agreed to defer their incarceration while they appealed the trial court's contempt finding.

The appeal by Fainaru-Wada and Williams seemed about as strong a case as the institutional press could have hoped to put before the justices of the Supreme Court. One important feature of their case was that it did not involve national security considerations that could color the arguments and tempt the Court to lean in favor of law enforcement. Another was that the stories published by Fainaru-Wada and Williams were not politically divisive, and were of unquestionable benefit to society. In fact, the two were praised by President Bush in 2005, when he told them they had "done a great service" with their reporting.

Any thoughts their case might be one that would entice the justices to revisit *Branzburg* were dashed, however, when federal prosecutors unexpectedly announced that Troy Ellerman, a former attorney for two of the BALCO defendants, had leaked grand jury transcripts, and had pleaded guilty to several offenses related to his disclosure of the documents. According to the Department of Justice, Ellerman had allowed Fainaru-Wada and Williams to come into his office and take verbatim notes of grand jury testimony, which they later used for their newspaper articles and book. After doing so, Ellerman told the Court overseeing the BALCO case that he had no idea who had provided the secret grand jury testimony to Fainaru-Wada and Williams. Following that representation, Ellerman apparently again let Fainaru-Wada and Williams into his office to take additional notes of grand jury testimony.

Although Fainaru-Wada and Williams still refuse to identify their source, soon after Ellerman's plea, prosecutors withdrew their subpoenas to the reporters, and asked the court to lift its contempt finding, which it did. With that, the legal arguments about the press rights of Fainaru-Wada and Williams became moot, and any hope that theirs would become a test case for the Supreme Court disappeared in an instant.

But there will be other cases, and an additional reason to believe the Court will revisit *Branzburg* is that the law regarding press freedom is badly in need of guidance from the Court. One of the principal functions of the modern Supreme Court is to resolve disagreements among lower courts about important issues, and to foster uniform interpretations of federal law—especially the United States Constitution. Although the Court has thus far declined to jump in and help resolve some of the confusion, when it comes to picking cases for review at the Supreme Court, the Shakespearean aphorism that "what's past is prologue" need not hold true.

The Court is an inherently conservative institution. Changes (in both legal doctrines and Court customs) generally occur slowly and only after considerable deliberation. Part of the Court's past reluctance to revisit *Branzburg* may relate to the fact that Congress has, on numerous occasions, considered enacting a federal "shield" statute that would protect at least some people engaged in journalism activities from efforts to compel the disclosure of information and material. Although enactment of such a law would not resolve any questions about whether the First Amendment itself confers special rights or privileges on the press, it would lessen the importance of answering that question, and would also render unnecessary many of the requests for the Supreme Court to recognize a

"journalists' privilege" based on "common law"—
which is judge-made law, set out in decisions rendered
by courts, as opposed to the Constitution or sources of
law generated by other branches of government, such
as statutes and regulations. That shield law legislation
was pending in Congress at the time the Plame case
reached the Court in 2005 may have been a factor in
the Court's decision not to hear it.

The Court generally also considers a variety of
other factors when deciding whether to grant review.
For instance, the Court is more likely to take a case
when it believes a lower court has erred than to affirm
a decision. The Court also evaluates the facts of each
case, and considers whether its procedural posture
makes it a good candidate for review. And, of course,
the Court can consider an appeal only when a party
has requested it—not on its own initiative. Therefore,
even when members of the Court think an issue is ripe
for consideration (or reconsideration) it can take
years for the Court to find an appropriate vehicle. The
Court often has to wait patiently for the right opportunity.

If the Court does reconsider the nature of press
freedom and the meaning of the Press Clause, what
*will* it do?

We have very little to go on. Before the death of
Chief Justice William Rehnquist in late 2005, and
retirement of Justice Sandra Day O'Connor in early

2006, the group of nine justices had operated as a Court for more than eleven years—the second longest period without a change in membership in the Court's history, and the longest since the early 1800s. During that stretch, the Court decided relatively few cases presenting questions about press rights, and declined several requests to revisit *Branzburg*. We therefore know almost nothing about the views of the seven justices who were on the Court prior to President Bush's appointments of Chief Justice John Roberts and Justice Samuel Alito.

We also know little about the perspectives of the Court's two newest members regarding these issues. Chief Justice Roberts was a federal appeals court judge for a little more than two years before being elevated to the high court in September 2005, and during that period he did not participate in any cases that offer meaningful clues. As for Justice Alito, despite his sixteen years on the court of appeals, the only hint we have about his views comes from a decision involving an employee of the World Championship Wrestling (WCW) television program, who produced tape-recorded commentaries played on WCW's 900 number, which promoted upcoming events, announced match results, and discussed wrestlers' personal lives and careers. The employee refused in litigation to identify the sources of certain statements recorded for WCW's 900 number, claiming his announcements, while entertainment, were also journalism, and therefore shielded from disclosure.

Alito joined an opinion written by one of his colleagues on the court of appeals. In it, they followed prior decisions of their court which had concluded that, under federal law, "when a journalist, in the course of gathering news, acquires facts that become a target of discovery, a qualified privilege against compelled disclosure appertains." Although the opinion identified this privilege as based on "common law" rather than the Constitution, it confusingly also described it as "premised on the First Amendment."

The court then proceeded to develop a test for determining who qualifies as a "journalist" for purposes of applying the privilege, ruling that "individuals are journalists when engaged in investigative reporting, gathering news, and have the intent at the beginning of the newsgathering process to disseminate this information to the public." They also explained that an appropriate test for application of the "journalists' privilege" "emphasizes the intent behind the newsgathering process rather than the mode of dissemination." Applying these standards to the WCW employee before them, the court, clearly skeptical of the arguments by the self-described "only real journalist" in professional wrestling, determined that the privilege did not apply.

While somewhat amusing, that decision does not

shed much light about Justice Alito's views on the nature of First Amendment press freedom. It concerned only a common law journalists' privilege, and did not discuss the Constitution, except for the vague allusion to the common law privilege being "premised" on the First Amendment. And even with respect to the common law privilege, we cannot infer much about Alito's stance, since his court had already determined in earlier cases that there was such a privilege and, in general, appeals court judges adhere to decisions previously rendered by their colleagues. As a result, we are largely left in the dark about Alito's outlook, as with the other current members of the Court.

If the Supreme Court does take up the meaning of the Press Clause, what *should* it conclude? Should the Court continue to treat the Press Clause as redundant of the Speech Clause, or recognize that it has some independent meaning? Should it reaffirm its view that freedom of the press is a personal right, and that its protection extends to all citizens? Or should it adopt a narrower view of "the press," and construe the Press Clause as affording protection only to certain people?

Several leading First Amendment scholars have recently advocated construing the Press Clause as protecting the institutional press. Echoing the vision of Justice Stewart in his speech at Yale Law School two years after *Branzburg* was decided, they would interpret the Press Clause as protecting the press as an institution, not the individual rights of persons or entities claiming to be press. Under such an interpretation, the government would violate the Press Clause only when it interfered with the ability of the press to fulfill whatever role that clause is thought to safeguard. The Press Clause would be seen "primarily as a protector of the institutional role of the press, and only secondarily as a source of individual rights."

I do not share this view. Although much about the Press Clause is subject to legitimate debate, we should be thankful that Justice Stewart's view of the Press Clause never took hold on the Supreme Court.

There is virtually no historical support for the claim that the Press Clause bestows rights on the "organized press" that are not enjoyed by others. Chief Justice Warren Burger recognized this in 1978, when he wrote that "no supporting evidence is available" for those "interpreting the Press Clause as extending protection only to, or creating a special role for, the 'institutional press.'" This conclusion is shared by numerous legal scholars, who have questioned the factual basis for Justice Stewart's assertion of special rights for the press as an institution.

Moreover, the notion that the Constitution confers special rights and privileges on "the press" presupposes the existence of an institution (or set of institutions) that comprises the press. In truth, the people are the press. Journalism is an endeavor, not a job title. Any one of us can engage in it, at any time, if we choose to do so. Stewart's mistake was defining "the press" as an *institution* rather than an *activity*— one that can be undertaken by an individual or group unaffiliated with any established organization, let alone a traditional news outlet. This view is consistent with the Supreme Court's limited interpretation of the Press Clause, which describes the press freedom as a *personal* right.

Justice White's *Branzburg* opinion recognized some of the problems with construing the First Amendment as creating rights only for the institutional press. In declining to adopt a constitutional privilege for "newsmen," he explained that "the administration of a constitutional newsman's privilege would present practical and conceptual difficulties of a high order. Sooner or later, it would be necessary to define those categories of newsmen who qualified for the privilege, a questionable procedure in light of the traditional doctrine that liberty of the press is the right of the lonely pamphleteer who uses carbon paper or a mimeograph just as much as of the large metropolitan publisher who utilizes the latest photocomposition methods." Moreover, he added, "the informative function asserted by representatives of the organized press in the present cases is also performed by lecturers, political pollsters, novelists, academic researchers, and dramatists. Almost any author may quite accurately assert that he is contributing to the flow of information to the public."

Many advocating special press rights dismiss the problems presented by having to define "the press" for purposes of deciding who gets such rights. Floyd Abrams, an attorney who has litigated First Amendment cases since the 1960s (often on behalf of large media organizations), argued in an article nearly three decades ago that "the press is entitled to a significant degree of protection specially designed for it" and, while acknowledging the "painful difficulty" of defining "the press," claimed that "the genuine difficulty in providing a totally satisfying definition should hardly deter us from affording protection to those who are plainly entitled to it." More recently, a large group of news organizations that filed a joint brief with the Supreme Court urging it to review the orders compelling disclosures by *Time* and the *New York Times* in the Plame investigation contended that the members of the Court who decided *Branzburg* had "overestimated" the difficulties in defining who is a journalist.

The trouble with interpreting the First Amendment's press provision as conferring rights only on *certain* people is not that the task is difficult. It is that the First Amendment, in the words of Chief Justice Burger, "does not 'belong' to any identifiable category of persons or entities: It belongs to all who exercise its freedoms."

Moreover, attaching constitutional significance to judgments about who is a member of "the press" would invite one of the few things we know the First Amendment was designed to avoid: conditioning of speech on the securing of a license. As Chief Justice Burger also observed, "the very task of including some entities within the 'institutional press' while excluding others" is "reminiscent of the abhorred licensing system of Tudor and Stuart England—a system the First Amendment was intended to ban from this country."

There is no licensing of the press in the United States because, "in a very real sense, everyone already has a license, and occasionally a duty, to act as the press," as Indiana University professor Jon Paul Dilts appropriately explains. Freedom to speak one's mind without permission from the government is a quintessential American liberty. We ought to consider the poignant question asked by one of the appeals court judges who ruled on the journalists' appeal in the Plame case: "If the courts extend the privilege only to a defined group of reporters, are we in danger of creating a 'licensed' or 'established' press?"

Justice Stewart certainly was correct when he observed that the intent and the structure of the First Amendment support the vision of the press as a check on the government. It does not follow, however, that any rights conferred by the Press Clause belong only to members of traditional media organizations. At most, Stewart's vision is an argument for extending privileges to all people engaged in journalistic *activities*, not for limiting press rights to the "organized press."

If anything, we should be more wary today than at the time of Justice Stewart's speech of the notion that the Press Clause entitles established news organizations to preferential treatment. The erosion of boundaries between professional and nontraditional journalists ushered in by recent technological developments ratifies the wisdom of refusing to read the Press Clause as creating a class of citizens with special standing under the Constitution. While Stewart might be excused for holding and advocating a narrow vision of the press given the times in which he lived, during which the dominant image of the press emphasized its institutional role, his outlook is simply untenable in the here and now.

When interpreting the First Amendment's speech and press provisions, the Supreme Court generally has been reluctant to make distinctions based on the identity or affiliation of the speaker, preferring to draw any lines needed based on *types* of speech. If and when the Supreme Court takes up questions about the Press Clause and the nature of press freedom, it ought to reject the view that people are entitled to special rights and privileges based on their affiliation with a particular kind of business or organization rather than on their activities.

Of course, to conclude that the Constitution does not limit the freedom of the press to one select group does not necessarily mean that the Press Clause is redundant. Perhaps the Supreme Court ought to conclude the Press Clause should be interpreted as having meaning separate and apart from the Speech Clause of the First Amendment. The text of the amendment itself provides a basis for reaching such a conclusion. Yet whether the Court moves in that direction does not appear to be of great importance, since the Court has demonstrated a willingness to broadly interpret the Speech Clause as encompassing most of the rights one might associate with press freedom.

If the Court reexamines the nature of press freedom, what is crucial, however, is that it recognize any special "press" rights conferred by the First Amendment must be based on *activity*, not *status*. As Justice Felix Frankfurter explained more than sixty years ago, "the purpose of the Constitution was not to erect the press into a privileged institution but to protect all persons in their right to print what they will as well as to utter it." If the First Amendment entitles "the press" to any preferences, those preferences belong to anyone engaged in press activities—the professional and the novice, the high-salaried and the volunteer, the dispassionately neutral and the unabashedly opinioned.

# CHAPTER THREE

# The Priority of the Press

Although the Supreme Court has yet to interpret the Constitution as treating members of the institutional media differently from other citizens, there
are many circumstances in which professional journalists are granted rights and privileges not available
to others. While these preferences take many forms,
most either allow access to places and information
not open to the public or provide exemptions from
laws applicable to everyone else.

Sometimes these preferences are extended on the

(mistaken) view that the Constitution requires them. Most often, however, distinctions drawn in favor of "the press" are predicated on the judgments of lawmakers, regulators, and civil servants that these preferences are beneficial to society. In some situations they are based on written laws or policies setting out criteria for determining who is entitled to special treatment. In others, press preferences are the result of ad hoc decisions by a variety of public officials, ranging from court administrators to police officers.

Preferential treatment for professional journalists is so common today that we often don't even notice it. Hardly anyone thinks twice when members of the press are admitted to war zones, crime scenes, or disaster areas off-limits to the public, or are granted special access to official records. We accept without question that in many government buildings, including the White House, Congress, and the Supreme Court, the press is accorded quasi-official status, with dedicated office space available to those issued "press" credentials, as well as specially designated seating areas for viewing official proceedings.

In theory, the idea of the government assisting journalists in their efforts to gather information and report the news is appealing. Whether we view the press as a conduit for informing the public or as a watchdog guarding against corruption and the abuse of power, we, as the public, depend on journalists. The extension of privileges to the press might be viewed as a kind of bargain, in which they obtain preferential treatment in exchange for advancing the interests of the rest of us.

In practice, however, we have allowed press preferences to multiply without considering thoroughly enough their purposes or the criteria used for their application. And the results are problematic.

It is clear, for example, that many policies favoring the press are rooted in misconceptions about the character of press freedom under the First Amendment. The overwhelming majority of rules extending preferential treatment to "the press" favor individuals affiliated with traditional news organizations or others who make journalism their "profession." This cramped image of the press is at odds with the First Amendment's vision of press freedom (at least as interpreted by the Supreme Court) as a *personal* right, which can be exercised by people who do not devote themselves professionally or exclusively to journalism. Moreover, the array of rules preferring the press over other citizens seems to ignore the view that the First Amendment does not guarantee members of the press any rights not available to other citizens. As a consequence, improper lines are being drawn between supposedly bona fide journalists and others engaged in journalistic activities.

The Internet is propelling a dramatic transformation of the way information, opinions, and ideas are developed and disseminated for public consumption. These changes highlight the need for reevaluation at all levels of government of the circumstances in which special benefits are extended to those we deem journalists, and denied to everyone else—an undertaking that should provide all of us a better understanding of the nature of journalism in the Internet age and the role of the journalist in our society.

## Press Preferences

The federal government and state governments have constructed an elaborate system of formal and informal preferences for those they deem "journalists." On rare occasions these preferences take the form of outright financial subsidies, such as the favorable postal rates first extended to newspapers in 1792, and later expanded to other periodicals. More often, any financial benefits are indirect, such as narrow exclusions from generally applicable economic regulations that would apply to news companies, as to all other businesses, absent the exemption. For instance, in the 1930s, Congress carved out news deliveries from overtime, Social Security, and child labor laws. In 1970, Congress passed the Newspaper Preservation Act, which relieved "economically distressed" newspapers from certain aspects of federal antitrust law.

Another type of indirect subsidy is exemption from having to pay certain fees owed to the government that apply to everyone else. One important example concerns the federal Freedom of Information Act (FOIA), which allows the public access to government records, subject to a number of significant exceptions. Signed into law in 1966, FOIA is considered a centerpiece of efforts to promote government accountability. It is also a vital tool for investigative journalists. Recognizing this, when it wrote the law, Congress decided that fees ordinarily charged for responding to an information request would be waived for "representatives of the news media" (as well as for educational or noncommercial scientific institutions, whose purpose is scholarly or scientific research).

While the impulse to ease the burden on the "news media" by waiving FOIA fees was commendable, the law problematically does not define the term. Disputes over FOIA requests are commonplace these days, with many requesters contending that government agencies suppress information with slow and incomplete responses. Some of these quarrels have involved the applicability of the "news media" fee exemption.

For instance, the National Security Archive (an independent nongovernmental research institute located at George Washington University in Washington, D.C.) has had several clashes with government agencies over its entitlement to the "news media" exemption. The first began in the late 1980s, when the Department of Defense refused to recognize the archive as a representative of the news media, and therefore refused to waive fees for the archive's FOIA requests. The archive sued, and a federal court of appeals ruled in its favor. After noting "it is not self-evident" what the term "representative of the news media" covers, the court determined that under FOIA it should be read as applying to "a person or entity that gathers information of potential interest to a segment of the public, uses its editorial skills to turn raw materials into a distinct work, and distributes that work to an audience."

Despite that ruling for the archive more than a decade earlier, in 2005 the Central Intelligence Agency began denying the archive FOIA fee waivers, invoking its own interpretation of the statute, under which a representative of the news media is "an individual actively gathering news for an entity that is organized and operated to publish and broadcast news to the American public and pursuant to their news dissemination function and not their commercial interests." The CIA defined the term "news" as "information which concerns current events, would be of current interest to the general public, would enhance the public understanding of the operations or activities of the U.S. Government, and is in fact disseminated to a significant element of the public at minimal cost." The CIA's stance is perplexing—particularly given that since the archive's earlier victory in court against the Department of Defense it has won two journalism prizes, including the 1999 George Polk Award and a 2005 Emmy Award for outstanding achievement in news and documentary research for its work on *Declassified: Nixon in China.* The archive thought so too, and in June 2006 filed a lawsuit against the CIA over its refusal to treat it as a member of the "news media."

As I write, Congress is considering the first substantive reform of FOIA in many years. Although the proposed changes are designed to ensure faster and more complete responses to requests for information, they do not appear destined to include clarification of the "news media" exemption. This would be a mistake. The mischief caused by the vague and narrow term currently used is sure to multiply in the age of the Internet, and Congress ought to proactively address this shortcoming in the law.

### Press Access Privileges

In addition to financial subsidies, many government agencies give professional journalists access to places ordinarily inaccessible to the general public. For example, the federal Bureau of Prisons permits "representatives of the news media" to visit its institutions "for the purpose of preparing reports about the institution, programs and activities." Although the bureau's regulations deny any intent to create a "special privilege for the news media," the rule clearly does so. The news media access right is limited to "persons whose principal employment is to gather and report news" for a newspaper, a newsmagazine, a national or international news service, or a radio or television program of a station holding a license from the Federal Communications Commission, where the primary purpose of the program is "to report the news."

Among the access preferences extended by the federal government to journalists is the right to visit select foreign countries to which other citizens may not travel. For instance, government regulations prohibiting travel to Iraq do not apply to "persons regularly employed in journalistic activity by recognized newsgathering organizations." Rules governing travel to Cuba similarly do not apply to journalists "regularly employed in that capacity by a news reporting organization."

Many formal and informal access privileges are granted by state and local governments, such as those extended to news organizations covering emergency and disaster scenes. California, for instance, gives public officials the authority to close areas to the general public when there is a threat to public health or safety, but exempts "a duly authorized representative of any news service, newspaper or radio or television station or network." Ohio has a similar law, exempting "any news media representative in the lawful exercise of his duties."

## Government-Issued Press Credentials

Another significant area of press priority involves government-issued press credentials, and the public relations infrastructure created largely for the benefit of select journalists who spend time working in government buildings, reporting on the proceedings. The federal and state governments spend millions of dollars in public funds each year to facilitate the work of these journalists, extending a kind of "information subsidy" to their regular press corps.

Below, I describe aspects of the credentialing process for Congress, the White House, and the United States Supreme Court. I have focused on these because they are substantively important. But they are also of great symbolic significance, since other government agencies and citizens take cues from these institutions about whether, when, and how it is appropriate to extend privileges to some members of the press that are not available to the public.

## Congressional Press Credentials

Both the House of Representatives and the Senate established press galleries for newspaper reporters in the late 1800s. Today there are three separate galleries in each house: one for daily publications; another for nondaily periodicals; and a third for radio and television media.

Those granted admission to these galleries enjoy not only special seating, but a variety of additional benefits, including workspace, access to equipment like computers, phones, and copy machines, and the assistance of a staff of federal government employees that provides information and support. Accredited journalists also have access to locations in the Capitol from which the public is excluded, and are granted priority over the public for seating at hearings. This perk is not inconsequential. Space at some hearings is at such a premium that people make a business of waiting on the lines for public seating, holding places for their clients, like lobbyists and lawyers interested in the subject matter of a particular proceeding.

Although numerous congressional press credentials are issued, not everyone can get one. They are allocated selectively, based on stringent criteria. And, for more than a century, this process has been overseen by other journalists. At the urging of some in the Washington press corps, the Standing Committee of

Correspondents was established to pass judgment on applications for admission to the press galleries and to enforce gallery rules, with the House signing on to the process in 1879 and the Senate in 1884. The committee has been at it ever since. While final authority on press credentials technically rests with the Speaker of the House of Representatives and the Senate Committee on Rules and Administration, the Standing Committee and the news organizations that run it are largely autonomous when it comes to accepting and rejecting requests for credentials.

The standards for admission to the three galleries in each house are similar. The Standing Committee of Correspondents is charged with limiting press gallery membership in both chambers to "bona fide correspondents of repute in their profession." The Senate Periodical Gallery also specifies that applicants must give their "chief attention" to the gathering and reporting of news and must be employed by "periodicals that regularly publish a substantial volume of news," owned and operated "independently of any government industry, institution, association, or lobbying organization." Periodicals published for profit must be supported "chiefly by advertising or by subscription"; nonprofit periodicals must be independent and "not engage, directly or indirectly, in any lobbying or other activity intended to influence any matter before Congress" or other branches of the government. The Senate Radio-Television Gallery is likewise restricted to reporters whose "chief attention" is dedicated to, and at least half of their income is earned from, reporting and gathering news.

The congressional press credentialing process has generated its share of controversy. This should not be terribly surprising, since the idea of allowing established news organizations to decide who may join them is a bit like the proverbial fox guarding the henhouse. As one might expect, the history of congressional press credentials reflects a propensity by the incumbent congressional press corps to close ranks and keep out rivals using new technologies. This tendency extends back to the galleries' earliest days, when the newspapers that originally ran the press galleries established rules excluding magazine writers, and later radio broadcasters. The original rules governing press credentials limited them to those whose primary salary came from sending telegraphic dispatches to daily newspapers. Complaints to Congress by the disqualified journalists led to the formation of separate press galleries—which is why we have three separate galleries today in both the House and Senate.

Predictably, this inclination to look skeptically at new media has resulted in struggles for several online publications seeking press credentials to cover Congress. The first Internet publisher mounting a legal challenge to his exclusion from the Capitol Hill press corps was Vigdor Schreibman, who launched the Federal Information News Syndicate (FINS) in 1993, after retiring from many years working for traditional news organizations. Schreibman, operating from his home, was the sole editor and reporter for FINS, which he distributed biweekly to subscribers by e-mail for a small fee.

While Schreibman had been issued press credentials in the past when he worked as a reporter for established news organizations, in 1996 his application for FINS was denied by the Standing Committee of Correspondents because he lived primarily on his retirement income and did not draw a salary from FINS, and because his publication was not published for profit. Some committee members also took issue with the content of Schreibman's Web site, with one asserting that it published "dense monographs" on the information age, rather than reporting news.

Schreibman filed a lawsuit challenging the rejection of his request for press credentials, but a trial court and court of appeals refused to consider the merits of his claims on jurisdictional grounds. Back in the 1970s, Consumers Union, the publisher of the monthly magazine *Consumer Reports*, had been denied press accreditation by the Periodical Press Galleries because it ran afoul of the requirement that "only newsmen with no connection to any lobbying or advocacy group can properly be admitted to galleries." The courts ruled that Consumers Union could not bring a judicial challenge to the denial of its request for press credentials because decisions about whether and how to administer press access to Congress were committed solely to the legislative branch. Adhering to that ruling, the courts reviewing Schreibman's claims concluded that decisions by the congressional press galleries about whom to admit (made with authority delegated by Congress) cannot be overridden without intruding on Congress's autonomy.

Despite Schreibman's lack of success in court, his efforts were not without effect. During litigation with Schreibman the Standing Committee of Correspondents adopted informal guidelines noting the "emergence of electronic publications as a legitimate extension of the print tradition," and stated it would issue credentials to online publications that met the same criteria applied to reporters from print publications. Using these guidelines, credentials have been issued to several electronic publications.

WorldNetDaily (WND) was not so lucky, however. Founded in 1997, WND describes itself as "an independent newssite created to capitalize on new media technology, to reinvigorate and revitalize the role of the free press as a guardian of liberty, an exponent of truth and justice, an uncompromising disseminator of news." It provides some original reporting, as well as links to other publications' stories.

In 2001, WND applied for, and was denied, a request for press credentials, on the ground that there was a lack of "significant" original content on its Web site. WND contested this rejection, taking its case directly to leaders in the House and Senate, charging it had been discriminated against on political grounds, with the committee acting out of disdain for WND's perceived conservative political orientation. WND also charged the denial of its credentials request amounted to a violation of its rights under the Constitution's press freedom and equality provisions.

For more than a year, WND showered criticism on the congressional credentialing process, pressed members of Congress to intervene, and also threatened a lawsuit. This considerable effort appears to have paid off. Nineteen months after WND's application had been denied, the Standing Committee of Correspondents reversed course and accredited WND, claiming it had reevaluated the Web site and found it contained a sufficient amount of original news content.

Although we do not know the real motivations underlying the denial of press credentials to Schreibman and WND, these clashes between established and nontraditional news organizations reveal some of the shortcomings with the existing criteria used for allocating congressional press credentials. Of course, if history repeats itself, a separate press gallery may be created for online publications. This would avoid having established print journalists serve as gate-keepers for their electronic competitors. But it would not solve—and in some respects would perpetuate—the fundamental problems with the process.

For starters, the idea that no one should be granted press credentials to report on Congress unless they earn their living doing it is both elitist and outdated. There will be increasing numbers of nonprofessionals engaged in covering the legislative branch for reasons other than financial gain. Journalism will be increasingly decentralized, carried out by people who practice journalism as a hobby, either individually or as part of group projects.

There are already a number of such projects underway. Several of them are receiving financial and organizational support from the Sunlight Foundation. Formed in 2006, Sunlight's stated goal is to use the power of the Internet and technology to "enable citizens to learn more about what Congress and their elected representatives are doing," with the aim of increasing government transparency and accountability. Since opening its doors, Sunlight has sponsored several initiatives. One is a project called Congresspedia, a wiki-based "citizen's encyclopedia on Congress" with historical and current information about the legislative branch and its members, the content of which is generated by visitors who add, remove, and otherwise modify the content, under the supervision of an editor. Another is the Congressional Family Business Project, which enlists citizens in a "distributed research" experiment to monitor members of Congress who hire their spouses and pay them with money from campaign contributions. A third initiative is being co-sponsored by a number of organizations, including at least one traditional news organization. The Exposing Earmarks project asks readers to help uncover facts about and study "earmarks"—sometimes referred to as "pork"—items in congressional spending laws allocating funds for a specific project, location, or institution (generally ones not requested in the president's version of the budget sent to Congress for approval). The potential of these and similar initiatives got the attention of *USA Today*, which observed, in a September 2006 article entitled " 'Blogosphere' Spurs Government Oversight," that groups from all ideological perspectives are using the Internet to empower average citizens and enlist them as watchdogs. Unfortunately, if some of the participants in these or similar projects sought congressional press credentials in order to attend hearings and press conferences, or have easier access to members of Congress, their requests would almost certainly be rejected.

Another troublesome requirement imposed by at least some of the congressional press galleries is that journalists and the organizations for which they work not attempt to influence the outcome of any issue before Congress. As an initial matter, it is obvious this rule is not rigorously enforced. Many of the parent companies and affiliates of credentialed news organizations regularly lobby Congress. Is there any doubt that Disney and General Electric, which own ABC and NBC respectively, as well as many other media entities, are mainstays on Capitol Hill? Moreover, this requirement is predicated on the fiction that journalists simply report "facts." In reality, many members of the press from established news organizations regularly take sides on issues before Congress. There is nothing wrong with that. If Congress wants to deny press credentials to people affiliated with or working for lobbyists, there are relatively easy ways to achieve that, without imposing a sweeping requirement of indifference among journalists under the threat of withholding credentials.

The credentialing process is also worrisome because entrusting established news organizations with the authority to control levels of access to Congress enables them to keep out aspiring journalists who do not comport with the mainstream vision of journalism. Perhaps having the press monitor itself is the least bad alternative, since it keeps the government a half step removed from the credentialing process. Yet the result of vesting news organizations with this power sometimes has been the exclusion of nonprofessionals or nontraditional journalists wishing to gather information about Congress for the purpose of disseminating it to others. This arrangement is likely to be more troublesome as the transformation and decentralization of journalism continues.

## White House Press Credentials

Like Congress, the White House grants press credentials to select journalists, which provide them access to events like briefings and press conferences, as well as workspace within the building. Two forms of passes are issued: permanent "hard" passes and daily passes.

Unlike on Capitol Hill, the White House does not completely delegate credentialing authority to an organization composed of journalists from established news organizations. The White House Correspondents Association nevertheless plays an important role in decisions about the issuance of permanent press passes. For instance, when the White House credentialed a blogger for the first time in 2005, it did so only with approval from the association. "It is the press corps' briefing room and if there are lines to be drawn, it should be done by the association," said Scott McClellan, then White House press secretary.

As with Congress, White House press credentialing has resulted in its share of controversy. At least two lawsuits were filed in the 1970s challenging the denial of a White House press pass or admittance to press briefings. More recently, it was the issuance of a press pass, rather than a denial, that caused a stir.

For two years Jeff Gannon received daily press passes as a reporter for Talon News, a now defunct Web site affiliated with GOPUSA, an organization whose mission "is to spread the conservative message throughout America." During that time, Gannon asked questions of the president and White House press secretary that many described as "softballs" designed only to demonstrate support for the administration and its policies.

In early 2005, it was revealed that Gannon used a pseudonym to obtain his press pass (his real name is James Guckert), lacked any significant journalism experience, and had a "colorful" past (which, some reports alleged, included work as a male escort). It also turns out he had been denied congressional credentials because of Talon News's relationship with GOPUSA. Given these revelations, and the perception among much of the White House press corps that Gannon had been functioning as a political partisan rather than an independent journalist, a firestorm over the issuance of his press credentials ensued. In short order, Gannon left Talon News, which itself later ceased operations.

The political and salacious aspects of the Gannon controversy understandably received considerable attention. Unfortunately, the incident was not used as an opportunity for serious discussion about the criteria used for determining who gets admitted to the White House press corps. In fact, in some respects, the reactions were a setback for press freedom. For instance, the furor over his two-year admittance to the press corps seems to have reinforced the idea that only "legitimate" journalists—that is, people from traditional news organizations—have a place covering the White House from the inside. Most reporters seemed to believe someone like Gannon did not belong alongside established journalists in the press room. Thus, in the wake of the incident, the White House Correspondents Association met with the president's press secretary to discuss ways to tighten up the press credentialing process. This is unfortunate.

More restrictive admission criteria are not what is needed. The White House already limits permanent press passes to those accredited by the House and Senate gallery, thereby incorporating all the prerequisites imposed by the House and Senate, which slant access in favor of established journalists working for traditional news organizations. Instead, what is warranted is a reevaluation of those criteria in light of the changing nature of journalism, and a proper understanding of press freedom as a personal liberty.

I am glad Gannon was exposed for apparently providing false information to the White House, which would itself be enough to disqualify someone from receiving future press passes, in my view. Beyond that, it is unclear whether there was a legitimate basis to exclude him had he wished to continue covering the White House and the administration. His reporting may have been biased, and it may have been superficial. But the government should not base decisions about press access on such subjective judgments, which risk injecting bias and inequity into the process. By making themselves susceptible to the charge that they were not engaged in authentic, valuable journalism, Gannon and Talon News did a great disservice to many current and future independent, nontraditional journalists interested in covering government and politics.

I am not particularly troubled by the fact that an inexperienced partisan was admitted to press briefings and got to ask questions of the press secretary and the president. Of more concern is the fact that, in the hands of the White House press office, pliable standards were applied to admit someone deeply sympathetic to the administration, when it is doubtful that someone with a background and credentials identical to Gannon's who actively espoused political and ideological views hostile to the president would have been admitted to the White House on a daily basis for two years. The incident should have been a wake-up call about the perils of allowing government officials to exercise subjective judgments when it comes to allocating press preferences.

## Supreme Court Press Credentials

In contrast with Congress and the White House, press credentialing at the United States Supreme Court has been uncontroversial, and remarkably informal. The Court issues "hard" passes to a small number of reporters (in recent years the number has hovered around thirty), as well as day passes that allow admission to the courtroom for specific oral arguments (the Court issued about 875 of these during the 2005 term, but many of those were used by the same person or organization on different days).

Like the official press corps on Capitol Hill and at 1600 Pennsylvania Avenue, credentialed Supreme Court reporters have their own office within the Supreme Court's building, as well as access to a section of the courtroom dedicated to seating for members of the press. Having reserved seating in the courtroom is valuable to reporters, since the area set aside for the general public is small, and allocated on a first-come, first-served basis. For high-profile arguments, the line for public seating can begin to form four to five hours beforehand (and those marble steps can get very cold during the winter months). In addition, until late 2002, those in the section reserved for public seating were prohibited from writing during Court proceedings.

While the ability to attend oral argument at the Court might seem inconsequential, viewing an argument in person is a different experience from reading a transcript, or even listening to a live argument on audio (which the Court sometimes permits lawyers admitted to the Supreme Court Bar to do when the courtroom is filled). It is all the more valuable because the Court is only gradually making its way into the twenty-first century. Arguments at the high court are not televised (although there are proposals kicking around in Congress to compel the Court to do so). In fact, for decades the Court made audio recordings of oral arguments but would not release them to the public. It was only in 2000, with the cases involving the disputed presidential election, that the Court first released audio of an oral argument to the public. Today the Court decides whether to release audio on a case-by-case basis, and has denied several requests without explanation. And not until October 2006 did the Court begin to make written argument transcripts available the same day a case was heard.

Surprisingly, the Court has no written policies or standards for evaluating press pass requests. The general practice for permanent passes has been to require a letter from the requesting journalist's editor or bureau chief. If one is supplied, or the requesting party already had a press pass from the White House or Congress, a hard pass is issued, which is good for the Court's one-year term. As of the end of the 2005 term (June 2006), it does not appear that anyone formally has been denied a request for a hard press pass at the Court. The criteria for day passes are less clear, and it does appear some requests have been denied— although I was unable to obtain any specific information about those circumstances.

Notwithstanding the relative quiet of the Supreme Court press credentialing process, one thing caught my attention. Among all of the reporters credentialed by the Court in recent years, Lyle Denniston unquestionably writes most frequently about the Court. Denniston has reported on the Supreme Court for nearly fifty years, working until recently for newspapers like the *Wall Street Journal, Boston Globe*, and *Baltimore Sun.* Since 2004, however, Denniston's writing about the Court has not appeared in a newspaper. Instead, he has been one of the main contributors to SCOTUSblog (SCOTUS stands for Supreme Court of the United States)—a widely read blog about the Court and the cases and legal issues before it.

When Denniston began working with SCOTUS-blog he believed, based on conversations with the Court's Public Information Office, responsible for press credentialing, that the Court would not extend press credentials to someone working only for a blog. Therefore, in order to retain his press credentials, he also agreed to cover the Court for WBUR, Boston's National Public Radio station. The Court's list of credentialed journalists identifies Denniston as affiliated with WBUR, and makes no mention of SCOTUSblog, even though Denniston does most of his analysis of Supreme Court work for that Web site, and only occasionally reports for WBUR.

The reluctance to identify Denniston as affiliated with a blog—a fact about which the Court's staff is well aware—seemingly reflects resistance to the idea that genuine journalism about the Court's activities can be reported on Web sites and other electronic publications. I have my doubts that a novice online journalist wishing to attend Court arguments and analyze them on a legal blog would have received credentials. It appears Denniston's experience as a reporter for established news organizations enabled him to retain his press credentials while covering the Court for a blog.

The Court, like many government institutions, still appears to employ a "we know it when we see it" approach to press credentialing. This approach is both unsustainable and inadvisable, given the changing nature of journalism. It is also sure to result in complaints from disgruntled nontraditional reporters whose requests for press passes might be rejected in the future. In addition, there is something troubling about the Supreme Court reviewing requests for press passes on an ad hoc basis, rather than by applying carefully crafted, publicly available rules that would ensure no citizen is unduly denied an opportunity to exercise his or her press freedom by observing and commenting upon the Court's activities.

## Government "Shield" Policies and Statutes

In addition to the access privileges afforded primarily to those working for established news organizations, other important preferences come in the form of exemptions from laws that apply to everyone else. For instance, the federal government has enacted at least one statute, and adopted a number of voluntary policies, designed to give journalists more protection than other citizens when the government is seeking to compel the disclosure of information—primarily for use in criminal investigations. One such policy dates back to 1970 when, in the wake of complaints from the press, the United States Department of Justice enacted an internal policy governing the issuance of subpoenas to "members of the news media." These guidelines (which are voluntarily imposed by the Department of Justice on itself, and can be revised or eliminated at any time) begin by recognizing that "because freedom of the press can be no broader than the freedom of reporters to investigate and report the news, the prosecutorial power of the government should not be used in such a way that it impairs a reporter's responsibility to cover as broadly as possible controversial public issues," and explain that they are intended to balance that concern with the fulfillment of the department's own responsibilities. The guidelines then set out a number of principles and procedures that have the effect of creating a substantially higher bar for the government to pursue information and testimony from "members of the news media" than from other citizens. Among these is a requirement that the attorney general of the United States approve all subpoenas issued to the news media.

Unfortunately, the key terms "news media" and "reporter" are not defined in the guidelines—and the department is left to interpret them on a case-by-case basis. One such case involved Vanessa Leggett, a part-time college instructor and aspiring author, who spent several years researching and investigating the 1997 shooting death of Doris Angleton, a Texas socialite. The case had all the ingredients of a true-life thriller: a mysteriously murdered wife; a wealthy husband, Robert Angleton, suspected of running an illegal bookmaking business, and hiring his brother to kill Doris; and a jailhouse suicide and confession by Robert's brother, Roger. Leggett planned to write a book about the murder, and conducted her own investigation, which included interviews of both Robert and Roger.

Although Robert had been acquitted of murder charges by a Texas jury in 1998, he remained under a cloud of suspicion and the watchful eye of federal prosecutors. In late 2000, those prosecutors initiated a federal grand jury investigation into Angleton's possible illegal activities. As part of the investigation, Leggett was ordered by subpoena to appear before the grand jury and to bring tape recordings and transcripts of conversations with the Angleton brothers and others, which she had gathered during research for her book. Leggett asked the court to invalidate the subpoena, invoking her First Amendment rights and a "journalist's privilege." The government opposed her efforts by, among other things, taking issue with Leggett's characterization of herself as a reporter. Although both the trial court and court of appeals merely assumed without deciding that she was a journalist for the sake of their analysis, they rejected her request, and ordered her to disclose the information to prosecutors and the grand jury. When Leggett refused she was found in contempt of court, and spent 168 days in jail—currently the second longest any American journalist has been imprisoned for refusing to provide information, and almost double the time *New York Times* reporter Judith Miller was incarcerated. Angleton, for his part, was eventually indicted on federal murder charges, fled to the Netherlands with false passports, and was later extradited to the United States and convicted of tax evasion and passport fraud, and sentenced to twelve years in prison.

Vanessa Leggett's experience is significant not just because of her lengthy incarceration. It also shows the mischief that can arise when government policies necessitate determining whether someone is a journalist, and the government has the power to grant or withhold privileges on the basis of its judgments. In Leggett's case, even though everyone acknowledged she had conducted her research with the intention of writing a book, and been published in the past (albeit to a limited extent), the Department of Justice never applied its own journalist subpoena guidelines in her case, and argued to the courts that she should not be considered a reporter. The DOJ's reluctance to treat Leggett as a journalist again reflects a prevalent, and troubling, view that only those associated with traditional news organizations are legitimate, and entitled to the special privileges.

Other government agencies have enacted similar, self-imposed limitations on their pursuit of information from traditional news organizations. A recent example is the Securities and Exchange Commission, which adopted a new policy on the issue in April 2006, following criticism from the news organization about a rash of subpoenas to their reporters. The SEC policy applies to "members of the media" and, like the DOJ guidelines, does not define this crucial term, which will dictate to whom its protections apply. Unlike the DOJ guidelines, however, the SEC policy statement indicates it is designed to "ensure that vigorous enforcement of the federal securities laws is conducted completely consistently with the principles of the First Amendment guarantee of freedom of the press"—suggesting the SEC may believe the First Amendment *requires* a lighter investigative touch when it comes to seeking information and testimony from "members of the media."

In addition to the kinds of self-imposed restraints adopted by government agencies like the DOJ and the SEC, Congress has extended some mandatory protections to journalists through legislation. Specifically, in response to a 1978 Supreme Court decision ruling that the Constitution did not prohibit a police search of a student newspaper at Stanford University for photographs revealing the identities of demonstrators who had assaulted law enforcement officers during the seizure of administration offices at a university hospital, in 1980 Congress enacted the Privacy Protection Act, which made it more difficult to search for or seize materials possessed by "a person reasonably believed to have a purpose to disseminate to the public a newspaper, book, broadcast or other similar form of public communication."

While these kinds of measures are welcomed by most professional journalists, many believe they do not go far enough, and that Congress ought to enact a federal shield law, which it has yet to do—a subject I will discuss further in Chapter 4.

For the time being, the most comprehensive protections for journalists are the product of state law, rather than federal law. Thirty-two states and the District of Columbia have enacted statutes often described as "shield laws," and as I write it appears Washington State will soon join them. Additional states have recognized some kind of privilege for reporters in rulings of their states' courts.

Although the laws vary by jurisdiction, in general they grant protection beyond that conferred by the federal or state constitutions by exempting certain reporters or journalists from having to disclose information they would be forced to reveal were they ordinary citizens—such as the identity of a source or materials collected during newsgathering. The laws apply in cases brought in state courts, as well as cases in federal courts where the substantive law at issue is that of a state rather than federal. They play no role in cases in federal court based on federal law, which makes them inapplicable to a great number of important matters, including all federal grand jury proceedings and criminal prosecutions.

The first shield statute was enacted by Maryland

in 1896, after a *Baltimore Sun* reporter was jailed for refusing to name a source who provided information about police officers on the payrolls of illegal gambling establishments. Nearly two decades later, New Jersey became the second state to enact such a law, and others followed suit in the succeeding decades.

The precise language of state shield statutes varies considerably. However, as a general matter, they cover only certain people disseminating information and ideas through specified media. For instance, some states (including Florida and New York) protect only "professional journalists" who engage in journalism for "gain or livelihood." Several others limit protections to those "regularly engaged" in collecting or writing news.

As for the media covered, few mention electronic forms of distribution—in part because most of the statutes have not been updated since online journalism became widespread. Some apply even more narrowly, covering only certain forms of traditional media. Alabama's statute, for example, which has not been revised since 1949, applies just to newspapers, radio, and television, but not to magazines. As a result, the efforts of *Sports Illustrated* to invoke the law were rejected in a defamation lawsuit brought by former University of Alabama football head coach Mike Price after it published reports of sexual misconduct by Price.

In addition to being outdated, most of the state shield laws fail to cover significant numbers of people engaged in genuine journalistic activities. This is because most apply criteria that are based on the professional status and affiliation of the person seeking protection, rather than focusing on the activity of journalism. One notable exception is Nebraska's statute, which provides a good example of one properly focused on function, rather than ancillary issues like whether someone is engaged in journalism for financial gain or at the behest of a traditional news organization. It covers anyone "engaged in procuring, gathering, writing, editing or disseminating news or other information to the public."

Most of the existing state shield statutes desperately need amendment. State legislatures should bring them up to date, so that they reflect the variety of ways in which journalism is disseminated today. They should also revise them to recognize journalism as an activity that can be carried out by people unaffiliated with traditional news organizations.

## Does the Constitution Permit Selective Press Preferences?

Chapter 2 explained that the Constitution does not *require* granting members of the press any rights and privileges not available to others. But are these press preferences *permitted* by the Constitution? Does it allow the extension of press preferences at all? Does the answer depend on how "the press" is defined, and the criteria used to determine who gets to enjoy them?

These specific questions are largely untested in the courts. Yet the relevant general legal principles are well developed, and provide reason to believe some existing preferences are problematic—and perhaps even unconstitutional.

The constitutional provision most germane to the legality of press preferences is the Equal Protection Clause of the Fourteenth Amendment to the Constitution, which provides that the government may not "deny to any person within its jurisdiction the equal protection of the laws." Of course, what constitutes "equal protection" is hardly self-evident, and it has been the task of the federal courts—particularly the Supreme Court—to infuse these words with meaning. The current understanding of the Constitution's equality principles and requirements is the product of thousands of court decisions applying the Equal Protection Clause to specific circumstances.

Reduced to its essence, the Constitution's equal protection provision applies anytime there is "disparate treatment"—that is, one person or group of people is treated differently from others. The amendment does not outlaw all differential treatment, however. Far from it. Instead, courts evaluate the nature of the differential treatment, as well as the government's rationale for it, to determine whether it is justifiable. The level of scrutiny applied by courts varies, depending on the nature of the inequity. Some classifications are reviewed simply to ensure there is a "rational basis" for the differential treatment. For example, a rule restricting driver's licenses to people without DWIs would only be examined to make sure it is rational and furthers a legitimate government interest, since the "class" of people with DWIs is not considered a constitutionally protected group. Other classifications, such as those drawing distinctions among people based on race or national origin, are given the highest level of scrutiny, under which the government must show that they advance a "compelling interest" and are "narrowly tailored" to further or achieve that interest. Also subjected to maximum scrutiny are instances of disparate treatment implicating rights that have been deemed "fundamental" by the Supreme Court, such as freedom of speech, worship, and assembly.

Even though professional journalists are routinely granted rights and privileges not available to others (including some people engaged in collecting and disseminating information and ideas), these preferences have rarely been scrutinized to ensure they are consistent with the Constitution's equal protection guarantee. Most press preferences simply fly under the constitutional radar.

There have been few formal, legal challenges to these preferences. Many people denied the privileges extended to professional journalists have accepted their fate without making a fuss, and we never hear a word about them. When lawsuits have been initiated, some courts have refused to hear them so as to not interfere with the independence of another branch of government—as with the challenges to congressional press credentialing. In the few cases challenging the allocation of preferences that courts have actually decided on their merits, the approaches have been somewhat perplexing.

In one case, filed two decades ago, Jack Jersa-witz, a self-styled independent journalist, argued he was improperly denied access to the Atlanta Federal Penitentiary to interview an inmate because he was not considered by the Bureau of Prisons a member of the "news media," which was defined as someone employed by a radio or television station with a license from the Federal Communications Commission. Jer-sawitz asserted that the government's regulation excluding him and other independent reporters from federal prisons unconstitutionally discriminated among journalists based on their employment status. While acknowledging the regulation granted a privi-lege to only selected categories of media, a federal court of appeals determined that Jersawitz's claim he had been denied his equal protection rights need only be subjected to the most forgiving level of scrutiny. Finding that the bureau's regulation was "rationally related" to its mission of maintaining security and order within the prison, the court rejected his constitutional challenge.

A year later, a different appeals court considered the claim of a television reporter, Bradley Stone, that Michigan's state shield law violated the federal Constitution's equal protection requirement by failing to include reporters for broadcast media within the coverage of the statute. Stone had been held in contempt for failing to comply with a subpoena to provide evidence to a county grand jury, and believed that because Michigan's law applied to some journalists, but not television reporters, it had the effect of denying him equal protection under Michigan law.

Like Jersawitz's equal protection claim, Stone's treatment was subjected only to the lowest level of scrutiny, because the court reviewing his claim concluded that no fundamental right was implicated by the failure of Michigan's statute to extend its privileges to broadcast reporters. Applying the least stringent standard for evaluating disparate conduct allegations, the court found Michigan's law passed muster because it was not irrational for the statute to cover only some journalists. Relying on a United

States Supreme Court decision, the court observed that a statute generally is not invalid because it might have gone further than it did.

I am somewhat puzzled by the conclusion of these two courts that no fundamental right was implicated by rules favoring some journalists over others—particularly in Jersawitz's case. The Supreme Court has repeatedly determined that press liberty is a fundamental right. Jersawitz was denied the ability to exercise his right to freedom of the press at the Atlanta Federal Penitentiary, while the Bureau of Prisons' regulations would have granted access to someone engaged in identical activities provided they were employed by an entity with a license from the Federal Communications Commission. The court seems merely to have assumed that no fundamental right was implicated, without any real analysis of the issue.

In Stone's case, the question is more difficult. In a sense, the court was correct that the "right" being asserted was immunity from a grand jury subpoena—a right the Supreme Court concluded does not exist more than a decade earlier in the *Branzburg* case, as discussed in Chapter 2. Yet the court did not even acknowledge that press liberty *is* a fundamental right, or consider the impact of Michigan's disparate treatment of journalists on Stone's press rights.

The short shrift given to the equal protection claims in these cases is emblematic of the almost total disregard for the equality principles implicated by press preferences extended to only some journalists. Laws and rules preferring "the press" have been adopted without sufficient consideration of the guarantees of the Equal Protection Clause, and the values underlying it. The failure to fully evaluate the equality side of the ledger when considering press preferences often results from the misguided view that only individuals associated with established news organizations are entitled to press liberties, and the belief that only professionals can be "legitimate" journalists worthy of such preferences.

Before the Internet revolution, the bias in favor of traditional journalists operated primarily to the detriment of freelancers and book authors, who frequently were left out in the cold, denied privileges available to those associated with established news organizations. Their exclusion never made much sense, particularly given that freelance writers and book authors produce some of our best and most important journalism.

Today, selective press preferences are even more problematic. Journalism is becoming less centralized, and will involve many more people than ever before—large numbers of whom will not work in journalism as a vocation. Every day the existing laws and rules for allocating rights and privileges to the press become more outdated and more unfair. We cannot continue to apply our twentieth-century play-book of press preferences to our new journalistic environment. If we do, it will be at the expense of the press liberties and equality rights of many aspiring nontraditional journalists.

Disseminating information and ideas is a fundamental right, and the government ought to have very good reasons to prefer some people over others when it comes to exercising that right. We have reflexively granted a broad array of preferences to a narrow category of professionals, largely on the basis of business affiliations. It is far from clear, however, that the government may permissibly extend preferences to only those employed by certain news organizations or engaging in journalism for financial gain, while withholding those same benefits to those undertaking precisely the same activities on their own or without the objective of monetary enrichment. We must begin to scrutinize laws and policies that expressly or effectively prefer established media organizations over others, and ensure they do not run afoul of the letter or spirit of the Constitution's equality guarantee.

## Other Problems with Press Preferences

Press perks are selectively allocated at all levels of government, in both the federal and state systems.

Bestowing such preferences to only some people engaged in journalistic activities not only presents constitutional questions, but also raises other concerns. Among these is the risk that extending preferences to only professional journalists may imperil press liberties by creating what amounts to a low-grade system for the licensing of journalists—one of the very things we know the First Amendment's Press Clause was designed to avoid. To be sure, our current system of press preferences is a far cry from the pernicious licensing scheme that prevailed in England, which the Founders loathed and sought to prevent. Yet our existing arrangements are not entirely benign.

When the government is in the position of deciding what members of "the press" are entitled to special rights and privileges not afforded to ordinary citizens it, in effect, gets to decide who is a "legitimate" member of the press. This obviously vests the government with the power to deny some people the benefits extended to others. But we should not underestimate the detrimental effects of having to obtain approval to carry out aspects of their journalistic endeavors on those extended the government's imprimatur and granted preferences.

One potential casualty is press independence, which can be undermined by fear that privileges given may be withdrawn, or by affording a basis for governmental oversight of the press's activities. The selective extension of governmental benefits to the press may also promote the kind of symbiotic relationship that can deter robust investigation and reporting because journalists (consciously or unconsciously) have a sense of obligation to the government in general, or to a particular agency or public official.

The mainstream press has long viewed the licensing of journalists as an evil to be avoided. Therefore, while numerous journalists proudly identify themselves as part of a "profession," a great many others resist the label on the ground that it might imply someone has the power to decide who is a journalist or set standards for journalism, just as standards are imposed on other professionals, like doctors and lawyers. Despite this, most journalists working for established news organizations readily accept—and even encourage—the system of preferences we have today, which bears an uncomfortable resemblance to the licensing schemes repugnant to the First Amendment.

And the problems presented by this pervasive system of selective preferences will only grow as increasing numbers of citizens unaffiliated with established media organizations engage in journalism. Technology allows more people to practice journalism without making it their career, and without the support of a traditional news organization. As the boundaries between professional journalists and other people engaging in journalistic activities fade, or disappear altogether, we should be more careful than ever in how we allocate press preferences, and mindful of the risk that under-inclusion is likely to result in the impairment of press liberties.

An additional hazard of selective press preferences is the temptation of government officials to consider the content of a journalist's or publication's work when deciding whether to grant press credentials or extend other benefits. Civil servants working in the press offices of government agencies often make decisions about allocating press preferences without the benefit of any written or formal policies, instead relying on ad hoc, subjective judgments about a reporter's bona fides. They ask themselves what seems a reasonable and necessary question: Is this person a legitimate journalist? This sometimes consists of nothing more than ascertaining whether someone seeking privileges works for an established news outlet. There are times, however, when the decision of a government official depends on whether the work of the person seeking a press benefit accords with the official's image of what constitutes genuine journalism.

## Reassessing Press Preferences

Despite serious concerns presented by our system of press preferences, the solution is not to do away with them altogether. "Journalism and a free press are among the most important human institutions of the modern world," Columbia University president and First Amendment scholar Lee Bollinger fittingly observed in remarks about the future of journalism education. It is not only appropriate, but important, for the government to enact laws and develop rules that encourage and assist journalistic endeavors, including creating limited exceptions to generally applicable laws for those engaged in collecting and disseminating information and ideas to others.

Nor should government entities be required to issue a press pass to anyone who requests one. Clearly, press preferences do not need to be extended to someone not actually engaged in journalistic activities. Moreover, on occasion there are physical limits constraining the number of journalists who can be granted a particular privilege. For example, there are a fixed number of seats in the Supreme Court, and the maximum capacity for journalists is approximately 120. In the rare instances when the government truly has more press requests than it can accommodate, we should use criteria for allocating those scarce resources that minimize the risk government officials will make decisions based on their own views about what constitutes legitimate or worthwhile journalism.

The problem with our system of press preferences is not that we have preferences, or that they are not extended to all citizens. The problem is *how* we allocate them, and the disconnect between the true nature of press liberty and journalism, on the one hand, and the prevailing criteria for dispensing press rights and privileges, on the other.

Preferences should be based on the *activity* in which a person is engaged, rather than who the person works for, whether the person is paid, or the views that are expressed. Many state shield laws limit their coverage on the basis of format—for example, to include only newspapers, magazines, and/or television. Relying on the format used to disseminate information and ideas as a criterion for coverage is increasingly irrational. When it comes to access issues, the "we know the press when we see it" approach to allocating press preferences is still pervasive. This often results in limiting press rights and privileges to members of established news organizations. Such an approach is no longer justifiable, if it ever was.

Admittedly, even a functional view of journalism requires definitions or criteria for the application of preferences. Some of the standards adopted by courts of appeals in applying limited privileges are instructive. One court determined that application of a journalist's privilege requires that the person seeking coverage had "the intent to use material—sought, gathered or received—to disseminate information to the public and that such intent existed at the inception of the newsgathering process." Another similarly found that "the critical question for deciding whether a person may invoke the journalist's privilege is whether she is gathering news for dissemination to the public."

Viewing journalism from a functional standpoint, and applying press privileges accordingly, is more consistent with the proper understanding of press freedom as a personal right, which can be exercised by anyone, at any time. No experience is required, no paycheck need be sought. Preferences based on function are also unlikely to present significant equality problems, since everyone engaged in a given activity should be treated alike.

Of course, thorny issues remain even when viewing journalism from a functional perspective. Is it appropriate to limit the application of shield laws to information actually published or disseminated to a minimum number of readers? Is it acceptable to deny press credentials to persons affiliated with organizations that lobby the government entity from whom a press pass is sought? What criteria should be used to decide who gets access to a government resource that is genuinely limited?

Reasonable minds can differ over the answers to these and similar questions. The clearly wrong course, however, is to keep doing what we have been doing—

instinctively treating only members of traditional news organizations as journalists, while viewing with skepticism anyone else interested in pursuing journalistic activities. We should be suspicious of efforts to allocate preferences that do not reflect the reality that we're all capable of being journalists now.

# The Transformation of Journalism and the Citizen Journalists' Battle for Equality

Although courts have largely ducked, and legislatures ignored, hard questions about who is a journalist, such evasion will be difficult in the years to come. Nonprofessional journalists are sure to occupy an increasingly prominent and significant role in American life. As the number of nonprofessional journalists expands, and their initiatives become more ambitious, there will be further challenges to laws that relegate them to second-class status compared with professional journalists and representatives of institutional media organizations. Many among the new cadre of citizen journalists will challenge and test court rulings, statutes, and regulations that deny them rights and privileges extended to professionals. They are sure to meet resistance.

With our pervasive system of press preferences we have created a journalistic caste system, in which those working for established news organizations are given priority over others sharing information and ideas with the public. Before the development of the Web we were able to hobble along, since the circumstances in which those not affiliated with traditional news organizations were actually denied privileges they sought were relatively few, limited to occasional book authors, documentary filmmakers, or freelancers. We can no longer get by with the current system—nor should we try.

Journalism is returning to its status as an activity rather than a profession. Yet the legal framework for allocating press rights and privileges is not keeping up with the pace of change. While nonprofessional journalists are multiplying in number and influence, they are often treated as if their journalistic activities are a quaint hobby rather than the exercise of a fundamental constitutional right—one that is vital to the effectiveness of our system of self-government. This needs to change, and change soon.

## The Democratization and Decentralization of Journalism

Supply creates its own demand. So goes the paraphrase of Say's Law, a principle of economics named for nineteenth-century French economist Jean-Baptiste Say. I have long thought there is much to the idea, and the relationship of the Web to citizen journalism appears to be an example of the theory in action. The Web is creating an overwhelming supply of people who want to share information and ideas with a wide audience, and there are growing numbers of people tuning in to read, and in many cases respond to, what they have to say.

But the rise of citizen journalism is not just about supply creating its own demand. Citizen journalism satisfies real needs. It is abundantly clear that traditional news organizations cannot, by themselves, provide all the information and analysis our society needs from journalism—a subject I will address further in Chapter 5. The limitations of the mainstream media are exacerbated by the fact that traditional news organizations are contracting. Virtually all newspapers are reducing their staffs. The *Los Angeles Times*, for example, has pared down its newsroom personnel by about 50 percent over the past several years. Television networks are doing likewise, including closing many foreign bureaus. Even successful ventures are cutting back—literally. The *Wall Street Journal* recently reduced the width of its paper, and the *New York Times* plans to do so in 2008, scaling down the space they have to report news. In this deepening void, citizen journalism has emerged—in a big way.

Scarcely a decade removed from the appearance of the first blogs, hundreds of thousands of nonprofessional journalists have taken to the Web in a purposeful effort to share information and ideas with others. Although many of them may not think of themselves as journalists, a great number of them are engaged in substantially similar activities as those who publish through established news organizations.

One segment of citizen journalism is composed of people in the right (or wrong) place at the right time. In recent years, much of the video and firsthand narratives from the scenes of terrorist attacks and natural disasters, like the Asian tsunami and Hurricane Katrina, have come from nearby observers without any preexisting plan to serve as "reporters," who take on the role when circumstances are thrust upon them. While the scope and scale of this work is new, its essential nature is not. Consider what is perhaps the crown jewel of American citizen journalism—the famous "Zapruder film." This recording of President John F. Kennedy's assassination was made by Abraham Zapruder, a manufacturer of women's clothing, while he was standing in Dallas's Dealey Plaza as the president's motorcade drove by. Zapruder alone among the spectators was able to capture the president's assassination. As a result, his unique footage became both a commercial and a cultural treasure. Initially sold to *Life* magazine, the film was later returned to the Zapruder family, and eventually "taken" by the federal government, in exchange for payment of "just compensation" of $16 million in accordance with the "takings clause" of the Fifth Amendment to the Constitution. Today, however, the miniaturization and affordability of portable video recording equipment makes most of us potential Zapruders. Recognizing this, established news organizations actively solicit video and eyewitness accounts from citizen reporters.

Were citizen journalism confined to these activities, it would be noteworthy but not of particularly great moment. But citizen journalism is much more than home movies of a tsunami or videophone images from a terror attack. It comes in all shapes and sizes. Some of it is episodic; some consistently produced. Much of it is the work of individuals; some, the product of collaboration among groups—many of them large (including, perhaps, Wikipedia, the collaboratively written reference Web site created in 2001, about which there is a reasonable argument that the fewer than 2 percent of its registered contributors who account for about 70 percent of its content are engaged in a form of journalism).

Citizen journalists collectively have become a force in breaking news. This is evident from examples discussed in Chapter 1, and reinforced on a regular basis. Consider some of the headlines from October 2006, the month during which Florida congressman Mark Foley resigned after disclosures regarding his inappropriate contact with pages working at the House of Representatives. Although the story gained traction after a report on ABC News, Foley's e-mails with pages were disclosed several days before the ABC broadcast by a Web site called Stop Sex Predators. The same week Foley resigned, reports surfaced that Internet powerhouse Google was in talks to buy the immensely popular video-sharing Web site YouTube. Again, the news first broke on the Web. This time on TechCrunch, a blog dedicated to new Internet products and companies, run by a former lawyer, who said he had received an e-mail that negotiations were underway, and that the price of the deal was $1.6 billion. Less than two weeks later the acquisition was formally announced. The price tag for YouTube: $1.65 billion (what's $50 million between friends?).

Nor is citizen journalism confined to one-off disclosures devoid of sustained coverage or analysis. Valuable reports about the conflicts in Iraq and Afghanistan, for example, have been distributed by nonprofessionals on the Web. Numerous other citizen-led investigative initiatives appear likely to rival work by traditional news organizations, or fill holes in their reporting. Among these are projects examining aspects of work by Congress largely neglected by the mainstream media, and others covering local news and issues.

Today, the majority of work by citizen journalists is done without the expectation of any compensation— and that is unlikely to change. There are substantial numbers of people willing to serve as energetic volunteers. While these volunteers may work without being paid, most are unlikely to take on citizen journalism projects that cost them money. Fortunately, the Web allows almost anyone to share information and ideas with the public at little or no cost.

Even so, some forms of journalism require financial support. For citizen journalism to extend into investigative work, and other time-consuming and potentially expensive efforts, the reporters will need money. The funding is starting to emerge from a variety of sources—including foundations, wealthy individuals, entrepreneurs. Even segments of the mainstream media are contributing to citizen journalism initiatives. Reuters, for instance, contributed $100,000 to NewAssignment.Net, a project to encourage collaboration between professional and "amateur" journalists, launched in July 2006 by New York University journalism professor Jay Rosen, with financial support from the Sunlight Foundation and Craig Newmark. Less than four months after getting underway, NewAssignment.Net recruited Pulitzer Prize–winning investigative reporter John McQuaid as a contributing editor.

Such collaboration between professionals and citizen journalists is a model foreseen by several journalism professors, including Jan Schaffer, executive director of the Institute for Interactive Journalism at the University of Maryland. She "envisions many tiers of journalism in the future, with citizen reporters doing 'small j' journalism such as meeting coverage, and professional journalists doing the 'big j' journalism that involves trend stories and enterprise stories based on ideas perhaps being culled from those citizen reports."

Many citizen journalism projects have floundered, to be sure. Whether specific endeavors thrive or sputter has no bearing, however, on the phenomenon as a whole. Citizen journalism is growing, and there is no reason to think it is a passing fancy, either in the United States or elsewhere across the globe, such as in South Korea where the widely read citizen journalism

Web site OhmyNews has grown exponentially since its launch in 2000.

Perhaps we should have seen the wave of citizen journalism coming. Some of the energy propelling the movement was discernible from the success of certain types of "old media" programs, even before the advent of the Web. Consider the immense popularity of radio call-in shows, or a television program like *America's Most Wanted*, which put its audience to work, harnessing the observational power of the masses. These were signs of a pent-up desire to participate and share one's views, which now has been unleashed by the power of the Web.

Citizen journalism is also part of a broader trend in which the public determines for itself what it wants to watch, read, or listen to, and when, rather than passively taking in whatever editors or producers select. Although little of what appears on Web sites like MySpace or YouTube could be considered journalism, under any conception, their head-spinning popularity makes it clear that the Web has transformed consumers into producers—a phenomenon recognized by *Time* magazine when it declared "You" its "Person of the Year" for 2006, and proclaimed to readers: "You control the Information Age. Welcome to your world."

Many of these heretofore unknown consumers-turned-producers will attract a sizable group of loyal readers. Americans are rarely reluctant to shower a newcomer with attention and catapult the formerly anonymous into the limelight. This has already happened with a host of bloggers, whose Web sites are regularly visited by tens of thousands, and who play an important role in shaping debate over policies and ideas.

## A Tempest Brewing

Changes ushered in by the Web, including the accompanying rise of citizen journalism, are taking their toll on established news organizations. "We're in the middle of a revolution," observed Paul Steiger, longtime managing editor of the *Wall Street Journal*. "The business models are being totally destroyed and reordered every day."

From the perspective of many within traditional news organizations, this is not simply a period of transformation, but also a time of peril. From one direction, the mainstream media perceive themselves as subject to growing hostility from government officials. This antagonism takes many forms, including public rebukes for decisions to disclose classified information, and increasing willingness to issue subpoenas to journalists and send them to jail in an effort to obtain confidential information in their possession—a trend some journalists believe undermines their ability to acquire information from anonymous sources.

From another direction, professional journalists find themselves in a strange new world in which their work is scrutinized by thousands of instant fact-checkers and critics, some of whom are becoming their competition. The days of the mainstream media as the "voice of God" are over, declared Dean Wright, a vice president at Reuters focused on the company's online, mobile, and interactive services.

Both trends call into question the long prevalent self-image of the institutional media as occupying a privileged place in society by virtue of its representation of the people—a claim that is difficult to sustain in the face of declining popularity with the public, and given the reality that many people are "representing" themselves by engaging in journalistic activities previously reserved for traditional news organizations.

Understandably, then, not everyone in the press fraternity will welcome citizen journalists with open arms. Many traditional media organizations and other businesses will resist conferring citizen journalists with the kinds of rights and privileges extended to professionals. Occasionally, the resistance will be overt and public. Mostly, it will be subtle, quiet, and behind the scenes—like the inevitable closed-door lobbying of government officials that will occur whenever changes to shield statutes or press credentialing rules are considered. But it will be there. After all, as *Daily Show* host Jon Stewart keenly observed to the professional journalists and politicians in attendance at the 2005 White House Correspondents' Association Dinner: "Deep down, we're both entrenched oligarchies with a stake in maintaining the status quo—enjoy your scrod."

Some nontraditional journalists have had success in their efforts to obtain privileges extended to professionals. For example, in late 2005 a Web site, FiredUp!Missouri, launched by former United States senator Jean Carnahan and others affiliated with the state Democratic Party, convinced the Federal Election Commission to extend to them the so-called media exemption previously reserved for traditional news organizations, which removes the recipient's spending from the reach of campaign finance laws regulating and limiting expenditures. In another important early victory for citizen journalists, discussed in Chapter 1, the California Court of Appeals rejected arguments from Apple Computer that Web publishers could not rely on the protections of California's shield law. Remarking on the "decentralization of expressive capacity" made possible by technological developments, the court explained it could "think of no workable test or principle that would distinguish 'legitimate' from 'illegitimate' news," and warned that attempts "to draw such a distinction would imperil a fundamental purpose of the First Amendment."

Some citizen journalists are running into walls, however. Kentucky was the first state confronted with a request from a blogger for press credentials to cover its legislature. The blogger, Mark Nickolas of BluegrassReport, was denied a press pass to carry out work for his blog, and was granted credentials only after he was subsequently invited to be a columnist for the *Louisville Eccentric Observer*, an "alternative" weekly publication. Referring to Nickolas's request, the public affairs manager for the National Conference of State Legislatures reported that the Kentucky legislature does not recognize bloggers as bona fide media and would deny credentials to anyone whose work appears only on the Internet. Other bloggers and online publications report being denied or otherwise frustrated in their efforts to obtain press passes and press credentials, and I suspect there are many unreported accounts of nontraditional journalists being deprived of press preferences available to those working for established news organizations. Examples of unequal treatment of nonprofessional journalists are certain to abound with the advance of citizen journalism.

This should concern even mainstream news organizations if we take seriously what they have argued in litigation concerning unequal treatment of some of their own. Consider the experience of the *Baltimore Sun*. In a lawsuit against the governor of Maryland, the *Sun* alleged that in 2004, the governor had directed that no one in the executive departments or agencies in the state speak with two of the *Sun*'s reporters. The *Sun*'s lawsuit contended that the directive unconstitutionally retaliated against the reporters and the paper for exercising their First Amendment speech and press rights. Although the *Sun*'s constitutional argument was rejected by a federal court of appeals (and the *Sun* did not seek review by the Supreme Court, presumably because it believed that if the Court did take the case it would likely reject the *Sun*'s claim that its First Amendment rights had been violated), the premise of its argument—supported by the *Washington Post*, the *New York Times*, Time Inc., CNN, and the Associated Press—was that its reporters could not perform their journalism activities without equal access to the governor and the executive branch of the state government, and that reporting based only on official releases and proceedings is of limited value. By the same logic, the application of more stringent credentialing requirements to nonprofessionals puts them at a disadvantage compared with reporters from established news organizations, and impairs their ability to perform their journalistic activities.

As for state shield statutes protecting members of

the press, most are woefully outdated. No state has amended its law in years, despite the profound changes sweeping across the journalism landscape. And recent experiences in the states that had no shield statute are not encouraging.

Connecticut, for instance, enacted a shield statute in 2006. Although efforts to limit the law's protections to reporters with journalism degrees were unsuccessful, the legislature elected not to expressly cover bloggers and other nontraditional journalists. While the statute safeguards information disseminated to the public through "electronic or any other means," it applies only to "news media." The definition of "news media" lists specific types of news organizations and their employees, agents, or independent contractors. None of the specific types of news organizations are themselves defined, and some are broad enough that independent or nontraditional journalists might be able to convince a court that the term applies to them. For instance, "news media" include any newspapers, magazines or "other periodical," or "news agency." More likely, however, is that the statute will be interpreted narrowly, to exclude many forms of citizen journalism.

In Washington, after a stalled effort in 2006 to enact a shield statute, in early 2007 the state's House of Representatives and Senate passed different shield bills and, as I write, appear headed toward an agreement on compromise legislation. Unfortunately, it seems likely that Washington's shield law will not apply to many nontraditional and nonprofessional journalists, protecting only those affiliated with entities in the "regular business" of gathering and disseminating news or information to the public or earning a certain proportion of their income from their journalism activities.

The experiences in Connecticut and Washington, and the fact that no state has taken steps to expand its shield law protection to encompass new forms of journalism, reflect a pervasive reluctance to recognize the role of citizen journalists and others outside traditional news organizations.

This perspective may also influence the Supreme Court, if and when it finally decides to take up the meaning of the First Amendment's Press Clause. David Anderson, a leading scholar of the history and meaning of the Press Clause, rightly contends that "deciding who would qualify for preferential treatment under the Press Clause would be fiercely contested, and is probably more legitimately contestable now than ever before, not only because of the multiplication of media forms, but also because of the blurring of lines between news and entertainment, politics and comedy, and journalism and business."

Most traditional news organizations are struggling for their lives, as the viability of their old business models collapses, and they face competition from other forms of media, as well as from citizen journalists. In his study of the history of objectivity as a journalistic ideal, journalism professor David Mindich observed, "when older news media are threatened by newer ones, an intense debate over the nature of news ensues, followed by an era of retrenchment and change." This transformation is underway. We should treat this period of change as an opportunity to rethink the nature of the press and its role in our lives. As we do so, it is obvious that the Supreme Court's *Branzburg* opinion was prescient when it expressed concern about drawing lines between journalists and other information-gatherers and disseminators, noting "liberty of the press is the right of the lonely pamphleteer who uses carbon paper or a mimeograph just as much as of the large metropolitan publisher." Citizen journalists would be justified in worrying that such lines will continue to be drawn to their disadvantage.

## The Coming Battle Royal: A Federal Shield Law for Journalism in the Internet Age

As I've noted, almost every state has established, either through statutes or court decisions, some kind of journalists' privilege. While these state laws are certainly important, they do not apply in federal court when federal law is at issue. This means they have no applicability in federal criminal cases or in civil cases brought under any federal law. It is for this reason that state shield laws played no role in recent high-profile efforts to obtain testimony from Judith Miller and others in the Plame investigation, or from the *San Francisco Chronicle* reporters who investigated and wrote about baseball's steroids scandal.

Because most important cases proceed in federal court, and are based on federal law, the absence of a federal shield statute leaves an enormous gap in protection for journalists. But the failure to enact a federal shield law has implications beyond a given federal case in which a journalist might want to plead for special protection. At the moment journalists are engaged in activity they hope will be protected—like seeking information from an informant who wishes to remain anonymous—it is impossible to know whether an effort to compel disclosure will be governed by federal or state law. While the existence of state shield laws might provide some comfort to a journalist and those from whom information is sought, both reporter and source must nevertheless recognize the distinct possibility that an effort to force the disclosure of the information they exchange will take place in federal court in circumstances where state shield laws have no relevance. As a result, newsgathering today transpires with the recognition it is likely that no journalists' privilege will be available. Advocates of a federal shield statute therefore contend that not having one largely negates the benefits of state laws, because sources and journalists feel constrained, knowing they are likely to have no protection since, odds are, any efforts to compel disclosures will take place in federal court.

## History of Efforts to Enact a Federal Shield Law

Congress first considered enacting a federal shield statute in 1929, but it was not until four decades later that the subject received serious attention on Capitol Hill. In the run-up to, and within the five years following, the Supreme Court's landmark *Branzburg* decision—in which it rejected the argument that the First Amendment confers on journalists a privilege excusing them from providing testimony to a grand jury (discussed in Chapter 2)—at least one hundred different bills were introduced that would have afforded some measure of special protection for journalists.

None of the bills made it into law, however. This was due, in part, to the fact that support from news organizations diminished somewhat after it became clear that Congress would not enact a law giving journalists an unqualified privilege applicable in all circumstances. Enthusiasm for a federal shield statute apparently also waned in the years after *Branzburg* when it became apparent that, despite the Supreme Court's ruling, a number of federal courts were willing to recognize some kind of journalists' privilege—based either on the Constitution or on judge-made law developed case by case (referred to as "common law").

It has become evident, however, that federal courts are willing to go only so far in fashioning a journalists' privilege—at least without guidance from the Supreme Court. At the same time, the voluntary self-restraint exercised by many government officials when considering whether to seek information from journalists appears to be waning. As a result, there has been a spike in subpoenas to journalists, several of which have resulted in jail sentences when the journalists refused to provide the information being sought.

### Recent Efforts to Enact a Federal Shield Law

After a more than two-decade hiatus, Congress again took up shield law legislation in late 2004 and early 2005. Sparked by the prospect that reporters might face jail for refusing to provide information to prosecutors investigating the disclosure of the identity of

CIA operative Valerie Plame, both the House and Senate introduced bills for a federal shield statute, and the Senate Judiciary Committee held several hearings on the issue. Although it remains to be seen whether either the House or Senate will push forward with shield law legislation during the 110th Congress, should they proceed there is reason to worry about the law they might enact.

For instance, the legislation circulating in the Senate prior to the 2006 election, the Free Flow of Information Act of 2006, reflected a lack of appreciation for the changing nature of journalism, and an apparent disregard for the rights and contributions of nontraditional journalism to the "free flow of information" that the legislation professes to advance. Specifically, it defined a "journalist" as a person who "for financial gain or livelihood" is engaged in news-gathering or news reporting "as a salaried employee of or independent contractor" for one of several specific types of media organizations or another "professional medium or agency." To qualify as a journalist, the organization for which the work is being done must have the "processing and researching of news or information intended for dissemination to the public" as one of its "regular functions."

The purpose and effect of the legislation were clear: to cover only "professional" journalists and exclude anyone engaged in the activity for reasons other than financial gain, including the vast majority of citizen journalists. Given this approach, it is unsurprising that the Senate Judiciary Committee failed to invite to any of its hearings about the issue a single witness vocally supportive of extending the proposed federal shield law to bloggers or other nonprofessional journalists.

Even if Congress is motivated to move forward with a federal shield law, the near-term prospects are questionable given that the Bush administration has several times voiced its opposition to the recent congressional proposals, including the Senate's version, with one top official from the Department of Justice calling it "a solution in search of a problem."

Although the 2006 Senate bill contains provisions mandating that the privilege would give way to law enforcement needs, a major objection from the administration is that a shield law would undermine national security by tipping the scales in favor of journalists, putting the burden on the government to show that it needs the information it seeks. The Bush administration believes the executive branch, rather than federal courts applying a federal statute, should make decisions about how to balance the needs of the press and national security considerations. The administration also believes a federal shield law would send the "wrong message" to leakers of confidential or classified information by providing protection for the journalists to whom such information is provided.

The administration has also objected to the conception of a "journalist" set out in the 2006 Senate bill, arguing that it is both over-inclusive and under-inclusive. The Department of Justice is concerned that the definition is too broad because it would encompass the media outlets of hostile foreign entities, and even terrorist organizations. At the same time, the administration has criticized the coverage of only those journalists working for financial gain at established news organizations, noting this discriminates against those engaged in journalism "on an uncompensated or unaffiliated basis." While questioning whether it is practically possible to reconcile the problems of over- and under-inclusion with the Senate Judiciary Committee's definition, the administration contends that the bill's under-inclusion would subject it to constitutional challenge on the ground that it unjustifiably discriminates against a category of speakers.

Even before the administration took a stand against the current shield law proposals, the effort to secure passage of a statute appeared to ebb. Proponents hoped that Judith Miller's incarceration would galvanize public support and turn the tide in favor of the law, finally getting it over the hump after decades of failed efforts. Those hopes were dashed, however, when Miller proved to be a less-than-ideal poster child for the cause. While in prison, and soon after her release, her reporting on a variety of issues—including the existence of weapons of mass destruction in Iraq— was the subject of intense criticism, including from within established news organizations. Questions were also raised about whether the source she purported to protect had offered to release her from her pledge of confidentiality.

The already uphill battle to enact any federal shield law also appeared to lose momentum in the wake of criticism of several news organizations—especially Miller's former home, the *New York Times*—for a number of stories revealing classified information that undermined national security in the view of many in the administration and Congress. And the cause probably was not helped by recent revelations suggesting the source for *San Francisco Chronicle* reporters Mark Fainaru-Wada and Lance Williams was Troy Ellerman, a defense attorney in the case they were covering, who Fainaru-Wada and Williams seemingly relied on and continued to protect even after Ellerman falsely represented to a federal judge that he had no knowledge about who had leaked secret grand jury testimony to the reporters. Before these revelations, many shield law proponents pointed to the fate of Fainaru-Wada and Williams as an illustration of why a federal statute is needed. With the disclosures about Ellerman's conduct those arguments dissipated, however, as some (including fellow journalists) questioned decisions made by Fainaru-Wada and Williams, and their case became fodder for shield law skeptics.

Although unstated, another factor in the administration's resistance to a possible shield law appears to be President Bush's view of the press. As with many presidents before him, Bush has no great love for the news media, and especially the Washington press corps. But many observers think his outlook is different from that of his predecessors. Like much of the public, Mr. Bush's administration appears to have its doubts about the claim that the institutional media represent the public. Journalists "don't represent the public any more than other people do," asserted then–White House Chief of Staff Andy Card, who added, "in our democracy, the people who represent the public stood for election." President Bush himself once responded to a question about how the White House's perceived indifference to the press might interfere with its ability to know what the public thinks by asserting: "You're making a huge assumption—that you represent what the public thinks."

## Enacting a Federal Shield Law That Protects Journalistic Activities

Congress should pass federal shield legislation, and President Bush (or his successor) should sign it into law. It is important to encourage the free flow of information for distribution to the public, so that the people have access to information needed for good decision-making and to watch over government, powerful corporations, and other important social institutions. A federal shield law would also send an important message, much needed in today's environment, about the vital role of an independent and assertive press in our society.

But a federal shield statute limiting its protections to "professionals" working for financial gain would do as much harm as good. Such a law would promote a view of journalism that is incompatible with the true nature of press freedom. In fact, it would set back rather than advance press liberty by embracing Justice Stewart's view of press rights—fortunately never adopted by the Supreme Court—as belonging to an institution rather than to all citizens. It would also send a terrible message to other federal government agencies and the states as they consider how to respond to the growth of citizen journalism.

Whatever version of a shield law Congress may someday enact, it should be the product of full and careful deliberation. This means that Congress should invite testimony from people with a broad range of perspectives about all aspects of the proposed law, including the critical provisions for determining who is entitled to its protections. The congressional hearings in 2005 and 2006 exhibited an absence of genuine dialogue about hard questions regarding the nature of journalism and who should be considered a journalist.

The shield law proposals recently before Congress also suggest we have a long way to go in convincing government officials that journalism is an activity rather than a professional affiliation, and that non-professionals have valuable contributions to make in furthering the "free flow of information." The view that the only legitimate journalism is carried out by those working for established news organizations will not be easily displaced.

An integral part of the claims that journalists are entitled to a "privilege" is the notion that they belong to a "profession." Many proponents of shield laws for journalists contend that just as other professionals, like doctors and lawyers, enjoy the benefits of privileges making it difficult for the government or others to force the disclosure of their communications, journalists are entitled to the same.

Consider a representative commentary—this one by former U.S. Attorney General Dick Thornburgh, about one of the congressional shield law proposals—published in the *Wall Street Journal* in 2006. Thornburgh criticized as a "serious failing" the "overly broad definition of who is a 'journalist,' and what constitutes 'journalism,'" complaining that "the bill does not require that a journalist be someone *professionally* engaged in the *legitimate* reporting of news."

Thinking of journalism as a profession is problematic, however. For starters, in the cases of doctors and lawyers, the privilege generally belongs to the client, and not the professional. Leaving that distinction aside, a great many journalists resist the idea their vocation is a "profession," out of concern that the label suggests someone has the authority to decide who is a journalist or impose standards or codes of conduct on them—as is done with doctors and lawyers. With the specter of government licensing firmly in mind, journalism organizations have been wary of relying too heavily on the notion they belong to a profession as the basis for seeking special rights or privileges.

Nevertheless, many established news organizations have lined up to support versions of the federal shield statute that would limit coverage to "professionals." In fact, lawyers hired by some large media organizations met with members of Congress and their staffs—and even helped draft proposed versions of the law.

The conventional wisdom among traditional media organizations is that a shield law will not be passed by Congress unless it focuses on protecting a narrow group of people. The position of the *Los*

*Angeles Times* is typical: "The day may come when Congress or the states will provide greater legal protection for bloggers and 'nonprofessional' journalists. For now, the priority is to make federal law at least as protective of traditional journalists' confidential sources as the laws of most of the states."

While this incremental approach has some appeal, it overlooks the fact that once in place, legal definitions of "the press" are exceedingly difficult to change, and existing beneficiaries of prevailing definitions have no incentive to expand the definitions to cover others. The reality is that if the most influential media organizations were protected (and advantaged) by a federal shield law, it is unlikely they would later push hard to amend it to cover others (who are, in some sense, their competition). Of course, an incremental approach also sends precisely the wrong message about the nature of press liberty and the role of citizens in disseminating information and ideas.

Ironically, such a strategy also appears unlikely to work. The claim to "press exceptionalism" that underlies many of the efforts by mainstream media organizations to secure special rights and privileges beyond those enjoyed by other citizens is hard to sell in the current environment, given their lack of popularity and the blurring lines between traditional news and other forms of media.

## Protecting Nonprofessional Journalists

Defending his paper's controversial decision in 2006 to publish information about the federal government's secret program examining international banking records as part of the effort to combat terrorism, *New York Times* editor Bill Keller remarked that "the people who invented this country saw an aggressive, independent press as a protective measure against the abuse of power in a democracy, and an essential ingredient for self-government" and they "rejected the idea that it is wise, or patriotic, to always take the President at his word, or to surrender to the government important decisions about what to publish. . . . The power that has been given us is not something to be taken lightly."

Keller is right about both the importance of an independent press as a check against abuses of power and the power conferred by the right to publish. Where most traditional news organizations veer off course, however, is in their belief that *only* those employed by such news organizations can meaningfully contribute to the effort. The view that professional journalists are entitled to privileges because they "represent the public" is widely held within traditional news organizations. And there is something to this idea—but not as much as mainstream media would have us think.

Established news organizations do not provide anything near "all the news that's fit to print"—either on their own or collectively. Even with respect to particular reports, people necessarily are not getting the "whole" story. Sociologist Michael Schudson is right when he explains that "news is not a mirror of reality." "It is a representation of the world and all representations are selective. This means that some human being must do the selecting; certain people make decisions about what to present as news and how to present it." Important information is omitted—sometimes on purpose, sometimes unwittingly.

Most traditional news organizations have always been for-profit businesses. Today, however, when the vast majority of established news outlets are owned by huge corporations, they are often serving their own interests first, and the interests of the public a distant second, if at all. "The notion of journalism as a public service institution aimed at the entire population has vanished," observed University of Illinois professor Robert McChesney, author of several books about the media, including *The Problem of the Media* and *Rich Media, Poor Democracy*.

From the standpoint of the Constitution, anyone engaged in disseminating information and ideas is exercising freedom of the press. This truth was largely obscured over the last century, as the tools for dissemination were concentrated into fewer and fewer hands. The technological, social, and economic transformation underway is reversing that trend, and provides an opportunity to reexamine how we conceive of journalism and the nature of press liberties.

Unfortunately, our legal framework is not keeping up with the pace of technological and social changes. We've seen that there is an extensive system of formal and informal preferences extended to professional journalists. Few of these privileges have been applied to citizen journalists, however, even when they are engaged in substantially the same activities as their professional brethren. We need a thorough reexamination of existing laws to debate how they should be changed to properly account for the reality that we're all now capable of being journalists, and to avoid relegating nonprofessional journalists to second-class status.

Some may question my call for change, wondering whether there is anything wrong with systematically extending preferences only to professionals, while denying them to citizen journalists. Is there really a problem? Why all the fuss when only a handful of people will want the same rights and privileges as professional journalists?

The importance of this debate should not be underestimated. Economists studying international trade use the term "comparative advantage" to refer to a country's ability to produce a good or service more effectively and efficiently than other nations. Although not a tangible object that we can sell in international commerce, one of our advantages as a nation is the remarkable stability of our political and legal systems (anchored by the Constitution), and the widely shared dedication to their integrity. Among the bedrocks of those systems are our commitments to freedom of expression and to equality.

Whether we recognize it or not, these commitments are directly implicated by the transformation of journalism underway. How we respond will tell us a lot about ourselves. Will we instinctively rebuff the claims of nonprofessionals seeking to be recognized as journalists? Or will we think hard about the nature of press freedom, and consider the equality principles at stake when we extend preferences not based on the activity at issue, but according to one's professional affiliations? Will we simply dismiss citizen journalists as "amateurs" lacking training and standards? Or will we ensure that any decisions to selectively grant press preferences are the result of careful and fair deliberation rather than ad hoc judgments and personal biases?

As nonprofessional journalists challenge laws and regulations that deny them privileges available to professional journalists and institutional media, I believe we will find that the disparate treatment authorized by such laws is often difficult to justify. In deciding what rights and privileges to extend to people outside traditional news organizations seeking to share their ideas and information with the public, we ought to focus on their objectives, not their methods, and on their activities, not who owns the vehicle they use to reach out to others.

"The era of hegemonic networks and newspapers" is "a memory," *New Yorker* editor David Remnick recently declared. My hope is that the rise of citizen journalism will elevate and complement institutional journalism, not undermine it; that all journalists will advance the public interest by acting as a watchdog over our vital institutions.

It is one thing to hold a personal opinion about the relative value of an article in the *Wall Street Journal* compared with a posting on a Web site. I am not about to stop reading my favorite established newspapers and magazines in favor of unfiltered information distributed by people and organizations I have never heard of—whether on the Web or otherwise. But the assignment of legal privileges and protections should not be based on subjective judgments about the legitimacy or perceived quality of the source of information or ideas. We must no longer accept uncritically the idea that professional journalists can be anointed with special perks and protections denied to others engaging in essentially the same activities.

We must also reject the notion that citizen journalism is less worthy of protection because much of it is not "objective," or because many citizen journalists advocate a point of view rather than dispassionately report only "the facts." The image of the press as detached and objective has dominated journalism for the better part of the past century. That image, however, is clearly fading—both within established news organizations and among the public.

While most traditional news organizations still adhere to objectivity as a defining characteristic of "real" journalism, most of these organizations have themselves undermined it by willfully blurring the lines between reporting, analysis, and commentary. Those lines are becoming sufficiently unclear that the *New York Times* in 2005 formed an internal committee to study the divide between news and opinion. The committee's work led, in September 2006, to changes in the paper's formatting that are supposed to indicate to readers whether the content is "objective" or "subjective." Unlike the *Times*, some news and journalism organizations are abandoning "objectivity"—or at least the term—in favor of other ambitions like "fairness," "balance," and "accuracy." This change has been underway for more than a decade, with the Society of Professional Journalists, the largest journalism organization in the United States, having dropped "objectivity" as a goal set out in its ethics code in 1996.

Part of the problem with objectivity as a journalistic goal is that its meaning is confused, and more theoretical than a genuine journalistic practice. This gap between aspirations to objectivity and the real world is not unique to journalism. In *That Noble Dream: The "Objectivity Question" and the American Historical Profession*, University of Chicago history professor Peter Novick offers a fascinating exploration of the fortunes of objectivity as a guiding light for professional historians. As with historical objectivity, journalistic objectivity is not a single idea, and lacks any clear meaning. It is a jumble of concepts and values. As a result, it provides limited guidance for journalists seeking to pursue it, or for consumers trying to figure out what to expect.

The ideology of journalistic objectivity emerged at the end of the nineteenth century as part of a broader cultural and intellectual movement. Today, however, consumers of news often appear not to demand objectivity in their news—at least insofar as objectivity requires neutrality and the subjugation of the journalist's own viewpoint. As explained by Duke University professor James Hamilton in *All the News That's Fit to Sell: How the Market Transforms Information into News*, objective news coverage is "a commercial product that emerges from market forces." The ideal emerged at a time when there was a need for news organizations to appeal to a large, undifferentiated audience, and the best way to do that was to avoid turning off large numbers of potential customers by expressing a point of view on controversial issues. In today's environment, with hundreds of cable channels targeting smaller audiences, and increasing segmentation of print audiences, the economic imperatives of objectivity are disappearing.

Objectivity is not an indispensable characteristic of journalism. Many parts of the world, including much of Western Europe, never adopted the emphasis on detachment and objectivity, and the bright lines between facts and commentary, that prevailed in the United States for the past century. And, as noted in Chapter 1, in the years leading up to our nation's founding there was no tradition of an impartial press. For at least half of the history of the American journalism, newspapers freely acknowledged that their judgments about news were influenced by partisan considerations.

Yet objectivity still has a hold on much of professional journalism, and many point to it as a basis for distinguishing their work from that of bloggers and other citizen journalists. The distinction is susceptible to exaggeration. Many established news organizations no longer even pretend to be neutral about the issues of the day. Others cling to a veneer of objectivity by offering "both sides" of an issue while nevertheless presenting a clear point of view. And even when journalists strive to remain objective, we appear to understand—even demand—that they routinely and willingly abandon their disinterested stance in some circumstances. We clearly do not expect balance or neutrality about terrorism against Americans, or whether the United States succeeds in its military missions. Most Americans would be outraged to read routinely about Al Qaeda's perspective in stories about terrorism. Thus, CNN anchor Wolf Blitzer showed little hesitation when he declared on air in October 2006, in response to a question from Lynne Cheney, the wife of Vice President Dick Cheney, about the network's stance on the war in Iraq and against terrorism, "Of course we want the United States to win; we are Americans."

Meanwhile, the picture of citizen journalists as a mob using the Web to spread uninformed views is a caricature, albeit a pervasive one. Although this image aptly describes many bloggers, few if any of such bloggers consider themselves engaged in journalism. In contrast, numerous serious bloggers demonstrate high levels of commitment to balance and intellectual honesty—in some cases more so than many mainstream journalists. There are also large numbers of initiatives underway to train citizen journalists and develop voluntary codes of ethics to guide their work.

While these initiatives are welcome, their absence would not provide a valid basis for categorically refusing press privileges to citizen journalists. Any journalist or journalism enterprise is free to impose on itself whatever standards it likes. But "objectivity" or obedience to any code of conduct is not required to trigger the protections of the First Amendment, and should not be required for someone to receive the benefit of preferences extended to the press.

Journalism is changing, whether we like it or not. We should embrace the transformation, and try to move it in a direction that recognizes there are important rights implicated by how the transformation proceeds.

# CHAPTER FIVE

# A World in Which We're All Journalists

---

There are numerous potential objections to conceiving of journalism as an activity rather than a profession, and to acknowledging that nonprofessionals engaged in journalistic endeavors, including some bloggers and other citizen journalists, are entitled to the same treatment as those affiliated with traditional news organizations. Below, I address some of the most important objections, and explain why they do not justify abiding with the status quo, under which a variety of rights and privileges are extended to professional journalists but denied to other citizens engaged in similar activities.

## The Problem of Line-Drawing: Everyone Will Claim to Be a Journalist

A widespread concern among those who resist recognizing nonprofessionals as journalists is the perceived danger of a slippery slope. They ask: If everyone is capable of being a journalist, and the government should refrain as much as possible from allocating rights and privileges to the press on the basis of subjective judgments about what constitutes real, or legitimate, or worthwhile journalism, won't we be overrun with claims by nonprofessionals that they are entitled to such rights, and won't government officials be left with little or no basis to evaluate the validity of those claims?

As an initial matter, I believe few people not actually engaged in the dissemination of information and ideas to the public will claim that they are doing so in order to avail themselves of privileges extended to journalists. In the event this problem did materialize, it would be perfectly acceptable, in my judgment, to require those requesting the benefits of a perk designed for journalists to affirm under penalty of perjury that they seek the privilege as part of an effort to share information or ideas with the public. This would weed out many pretenders, and go a long way toward guarding against boundless expansion of press privileges.

This leaves the questions whether we should be concerned with line-drawing challenges posed by expanding the group of people entitled to special rights and privileges conferred on those actually engaged in journalism activities, and whether such concerns could justify maintaining our restrictive views of who qualifies as a journalist.

Suggestions that letting go of our narrow conception of journalism will result in intolerable uncertainty about who is a journalist seem to ignore that we already face difficult line-drawing questions today, and have for some time. The questions may have seemed easy to some, because the criteria used to allocate rights and privileges have typically defined journalists as only those employed by established news organizations. But there have been challenging questions even under the prevailing, narrow conception of journalism, as evidenced by the many court cases struggling to apply state shield statutes.

In addition, allocating press preferences based on a functional view of journalism does not mean we would be without criteria to evaluate (and limit) claims of entitlement to rights and privileges designed for journalists. It would be defensible to limit privileges to those who add some original analysis or content to what they disseminate to the public, which would exclude those who merely aggregate content created entirely by others. Moreover, in the rare situations where there are physical constraints on the number of people who can receive a preference—such as limited seating in a courtroom—the government can use a number of neutral criteria to decide which journalists will receive it, such as a lottery system or a first-come, first-served rule.

Admittedly, even with a functional approach to the allocation of press preferences, there would still be difficult judgments to make when evaluating specific claims of entitlement. But we must move the baseline. Today, nonprofessionals are categorically excluded from many laws and rules conferring press preferences. Any line-drawing challenges should involve hard questions about whether someone is actually engaged in disseminating information and ideas to the public, not whether someone is sufficiently affiliated with an established news organization or earns enough income from reporting to qualify for a journalists' privilege.

Moreover, we must not lose sight of the fact that the allocation of press preferences implicates constitutional rights and principles. Even if line-drawing were made more complicated by adopting a broader conception of journalism, that would be a small price to pay. If we err in our line-drawing, over-extension of preferences is far preferable to denying press privileges to people actually engaged in the practice of journalism.

## Extending Protections Will Result in Fewer Rights for All of Us

Another serious objection to a broad conception of journalism is the idea that it will result in *fewer* rights for everyone rather than *more* rights for citizen journalists. This concern is expressed by many traditional news organizations (and their lawyers), as well as by some academics. Floyd Abrams, a leading First Amendment lawyer who regularly represents traditional news organizations, has asserted with respect to the effort to secure a federal journalists' privilege that "if everybody's entitled to the privilege, nobody will get it." Fred Schauer, a First Amendment scholar at Harvard's Kennedy School of Government, is similarly concerned about what he views as "institutional agnosticism" in the Supreme Court's vision of the First Amendment, under which, he believes, the Court's reluctance to draw boundaries around the institutional press has resulted in fewer press rights under the Constitution. "A Supreme Court unwilling to distinguish among the lone pamphleteer, the blogger, and the full-time reporter for the *New York Times* is far less likely to grant special privileges to pamphleteers and bloggers than it is, as it has, to grant privileges to no one," he contends.

I must concede that, in the short run, there is something to this argument—at least when it comes to the discretionary allocation of preferences to journalists by the government (as opposed to rights that are required by the federal Constitution or state constitutions). Consider the prospects for a federal shield statute, discussed in Chapter 4. There is undeniable resistance from many legislators to an expansive conception of journalism in a potential new law.

This concern should abate over time, however, if we can change the way we view press liberty and journalism. If we understand journalism as an activity rather than an occupation, and press liberty as a right that belongs to every individual, rather than to a narrow set of established institutions, the political calculus influencing who is protected by a federal shield statute would likely change, and legislators should become more willing to abandon their constricted views of what qualifies as a journalistic activity worthy of protection. For the moment, members of Congress appear principally concerned about the views of mainstream media organizations. But if bloggers and other citizen journalists stand up and demand to have their interests taken into account, that should improve the prospects for a federal shield law based on a functional view of journalism.

As for the courts, and their interpretation of the Press Clause, the several-decades effort by established news organizations to convince the federal courts that the First Amendment confers rights on them that are not enjoyed by others has largely been a failure. The Supreme Court has not retreated from its view of press freedom as an individual right, and its recognition that press activity can take many forms, and can occur outside mainstream news organizations. Urging the Supreme Court to adhere to an expansive view of journalism and press liberty whenever it revisits the Press Clause, or considers whether to develop a judge-made common law privilege, which it is authorized by Congress to do, should not result in fewer rights for anyone. It also might help displace pervasive misconceptions about the nature of press freedom that result in systemic preferential treatment for professional journalists and the denial of similar privileges for many nontraditional journalists.

## Undermining the Watchdog Function of the Press

As discussed in Chapter 2, one of the central roles of the press is its watchdog function, in which it looks out for, and exposes, abuses of power and corruption. Will a broader view of journalism and press freedom somehow discourage watchdog journalism or undermine its efficacy? It is difficult to see how, but there are two related and somewhat plausible arguments.

The first is that embracing a more expansive conception of journalism and the press will exacerbate the economic troubles of traditional news organizations, by further diverting readers and advertisers to nontraditional sources of information. In so doing, it will deprive those organizations of the financial resources required for the kind of reporting that serves as a check against government waste, corruption, and abuse.

The second argument is that considering potentially everyone a journalist belittles what the professionals do, and ultimately will result in their devaluation by society. This too will aggravate the financial woes of news organizations that historically have devoted much of the time and money necessary for the press to fulfill its watchdog function.

Although we ought to be concerned with potential impairment of the press's collective performance as a watchdog, I do not believe adopting a broader conception of journalism or expanding the universe of those entitled to press preferences will undermine watchdog activities. To the contrary, they are likely to improve them.

We can agree that mainstream news organizations do not perform their watchdog functions perfectly. Almost all of them are for-profit corporations, increasingly focused on the bottom line. Unfortunately, the financial rewards are often limited for the thorough, time-consuming, and sometimes dry work at the core of the watchdog function. As a result, the news ethic that once propelled these organizations is being displaced by a focus on dollars and cents, and by a resultant shift toward entertainment and superficiality over investigation and analysis.

There are also scores of issues about which there is disturbingly little or no coverage. International affairs have suffered from serious neglect in recent years. Another critically important area that receives sparse attention is state and local government, which television news almost entirely ignores, and newspapers seem to cover less and less.

But even when traditional news organizations dedicate significant resources to important stories, they often perform poorly. Consider the lead-up to the war in Iraq. No one could accuse leading newspapers of having assigned too few reporters to cover the impending conflict. The problem, instead, was *how* they covered it. Many news organizations, including the *New York Times* and *Washington Post*, conceded several years after the inception of the war that they failed to adequately scrutinize the justification for military action. Although this is among the most glaring examples of the failure to dig deep and ask tough questions, it is by no means unique.

The light touch sometimes used by established news organizations is attributable, in part, to the interdependence between government officials and the reporters who regularly cover them. This interdependence was in plain view at the recent trial of Scooter Libby, during which reporters and government officials testified about their reliance on one another.

Michael Schudson observes that "political institutions and media institutions are so deeply intertwined, so thoroughly engaged in a complex dance with each other, that it is not easy to distinguish where one begins and the other leaves off." As a result, "news is as much a product of sources as of journalists," in his view. Senate historian Donald Ritchie, the author of two books on the Washington press corps, similarly concludes that "the historical relationship between press and politicians in Washington has been far more intimate than adversarial," and he likens it to a "state of mutual benefit or mutual seduction." "The news media can be and are used as an extension of government and officials at least as much as a check," notes Timothy Cook of Louisiana State University in *Governing with the News*, his analysis of the media as a kind of political institution. Two other journalism professors recently found "stunning gaps" that "suggest the hesitancy or inability of news organizations to act systematically or routinely as watchdogs in covering other matters of high importance."

Similar problems plague coverage of nongovernmental institutions and organizations. Schudson uses the term "parajournalists" to refer to the public relations firms, public information officers, and publicity staffs of both corporate and nonprofit institutions who feed information to employees of traditional news organizations. Much of what we think of as "news," in his view, is the result of interaction between journalists and parajournalists.

When it comes to ferreting out corporate malfeasance, the mainstream media have demonstrated limited will or ability. Most coverage of publicly traded corporations is superficial, at best. Business journalists played a limited role in uncovering the recent wave of corporate scandals, like Enron and World-Com, and primarily reacted to the stories after they broke, even though publicly available information should have given rise to many questions that were never asked.

Clearly, for a variety of reasons, traditional news organizations often fail to fulfill their watchdog potential. We should therefore welcome, rather than resist, the contributions of citizen journalists. If anything, adding voices from outside the mainstream

should enhance rather than diminish watchdog journalism.

The power of public scrutiny in our society cannot
be underestimated. As renowned publisher Joseph
Pulitzer said more than a century ago: "More crime,
immorality and rascality is prevented by fear of exposure in the newspapers than by all of the laws, moral
and statute ever devised." Today, potential exposure
is not confined to coverage by traditional news organizations. We should harness the power of the citizen
journalism movement to promote accountability and
transparency at our most important government and
social institutions by encouraging more people to
watch over them, and share what they find with
others.

And there is every reason to think that individuals and organizations other than established news
organizations can serve as effective watchdogs.

Bloggers and other nontraditional journalists are
arguably much more in line with the legacy of Revo-
lutionary-era pamphleteers than today's mainstream
journalists, most of whom work at for-profit media
giants, and often have a symbiotic relationship with
the government officials they cover. The Supreme
Court seemed to recognize this a decade ago when it
observed, in a 1997 decision concerning obscene and
indecent online communications, that through the
Internet anyone can become "a town crier" or a

"pamphleteer." That some of the work by nontraditional journalists may be anonymous does not render it unauthentic journalism. As the Court also noted, almost a half century ago, "anonymous pamphlets, leaflets, brochures and even books have played an important role in the progress of mankind." More recently, in striking down an Ohio law that forbade the distribution of anonymous campaign literature, the Court declared that "an author's decision to remain anonymous . . . is an aspect of the freedom of speech protected by the First Amendment."

Even before the Web, independent journalists like I. F. Stone, who in some respects is a forerunner of bloggers, publishing an independent political and investigative newsletter, *I. F. Stone's Weekly*, for two decades, effectively questioned and challenged government policies, including activity during the Vietnam War. Important investigative journalism is also being conducted, both before and since the development of the Web, by organizations unaffiliated with traditional news establishments—for example, by public interest groups like the Center for Public Integrity and nonprofits like the World Security Institute, which focuses on foreign affairs.

Citizen journalism is a natural extension of these individual and collective efforts, and we should expect and encourage them to grow in number and breadth.

## Undermining the Screening, Sorting, and Agenda-Setting Functions of the Press

Before the advent of the Web, the press would wade through vast amounts of news and information and decide what was significant enough to share with the public. Traditional news organizations thereby performed a sorting function—referred to by some media scholars as "agenda-setting"—signaling to their readers when something was sufficiently important for them to care about.

The days of traditional news organizations as gatekeepers of information are nearly over. Today, even an individual with limited financial resources has access to vast amounts of information, through publicly available databases and Web sites organized and maintained by a variety of government agencies and private organizations, much of which was formerly accessible only to journalists and select others, if at all. In addition, the millions of individuals formerly confined to the role of consumers of what traditional news organizations put out are now sharing their considerable knowledge with others—many of whom break "news" that triggers follow-up from established news outlets.

We are overwhelmed with data and information. In the view of some, in this environment the press's sorting and agenda-setting functions are more important than ever. If we expand our view of journalism, will we be left with a lot of noise but a diminished collective ability to distinguish fact from assertion, the significant from the trivial?

Yes, the development of a robust citizen journalism movement will deprive the mainstream media of its near monopoly over agenda-setting for public discussion and debate. They will have to share that role with their former audience. That, however, is a positive development, not cause for alarm. Traditional news organizations will almost certainly continue to play a preeminent role in determining what issues receive considerable public attention. But the evidence is clear that they suffer from shortcomings, and apparently can use some help when it comes to sorting and agenda-setting.

As the distinctions between news and entertainment have virtually collapsed, news has become a largely commercial product. The vast majority of established media organizations—particularly television news—promote the sensational and the novel, while ignoring the important and the complex. This trend was on full display on August 17, 2006, the day a federal judge declared one of President Bush's wiretapping programs unconstitutional—an event that received astoundingly little attention in the mainstream media, which instead broadcast seemingly endless coverage of the arrest in Thailand the day prior of John Mark Karr, at the time a suspect in the 1996 murder of six-year-old JonBenet Ramsey.

Established news organizations also make serious mistakes. Whatever quality control measures established news organizations have in place—efforts that are both important and welcome—they do not prevent errors. Nor do they prevent occasional wholesale frauds, such as those perpetrated on readers by the likes of Stephen Glass, Janet Cooke, and Jayson Blair, all rising journalism stars before their fabrications were discovered.

From time to time the mistakes of mainstream news organizations result in the payment of libel settlements and judgments. Remember Richard Jewell, all-but-shackled by some news outlets as allegedly responsible for the1996 bombing at Atlanta's Centennial Olympic Park?

The mainstream media also tend to report about the same events and issues. Citizen journalists' most significant contribution may be to expand what is covered. After all, they are likely to know better than professional journalists what is on their mind, and what is being neglected that warrants attention.

Still, when it comes to information, do we simply have too many options in the Internet age? In *The Paradox of Choice*, Barry Schwartz examines the proliferation of options we face when selecting among goods and services, and argues that at some point the choices become potentially debilitating and diminish rather than contribute to our overall welfare. Although Schwartz does not address information alternatives generally, or news sources in particular, his overall assessment of "choice overload" is compelling, and one might borrow his analysis to support the claim that, when it comes to journalism, less just might be more.

I am skeptical, however, that, when it comes to information and the number of people analyzing it, less is more. Although it may be considerably more difficult today for consumers to decide where to turn for news and analysis of events than it was a few decades ago when options were relatively few, this does not mean we will be left paralyzed by an overwhelming array of choices. Although I leave the technological details to others, I expect intrepid entrepreneurs are busily working on technology to help consumers sort through the vast amounts of information, analysis, and commentary on the Internet. One recently launched project along these lines is NewsTrust, a nonprofit online news rating system designed "to help people identify quality journalism." Just as Google and other search engines helped bring order to the Web, future innovations may enable us to rate and rank new and/or independent news sources for accuracy and interest, similar to the way sellers are classified by buyers on eBay and Amazon.com.

In any event, neither the fact that we are awash in information, nor any curtailment of the press's role as an agenda-setter, could justify maintaining a narrow view of the press that denies nonprofessionals engaged in journalism activities the rights and privileges extended to those working for established news organizations. First Amendment and equality principles cannot be cast aside in order to preserve the pre-eminent place of traditional news organizations.

## The Future of Journalism

Journalism is essential. It is a vital part of the way we create and share information needed for the functioning of our political and economic systems. We all have an interest in ensuring the maintenance of a vibrant and free press.

It is therefore understandable that the current condition of journalism is a source of grave concern to many, and consideration of its future a cause of anxiety. The economics of the news business is being turned upside down, leading to a massive reorganization of resources and ever-changing strategies to keep up with the pace of change.

What the news business puts out is changing too. Although written in 1999—a technological lifetime ago—James Gleick's *Faster: The Acceleration of Just*

*About Everything* is a poignant account of our in-creasingly frantic lives and contracting attention spans. It seems that we want our news like every-thing else: faster. What used to be described as the "news cycle" has quickened to the point where there is no "cycle" at all, only the moment—a process that began in earnest with the advent of twenty-four-hour cable news and culminated with the widespread use of the Web.

We also appear to want our news lighter—less detailed and less serious. Programming and reporting about the nitty-gritty of government, the details of the business world, or the underbelly of social problems, simply do not attract large audiences. Because they do not, news organizations are less inclined to produce them. Instead, most of our "news" looks like just another form of content. Journalism is losing its dis-tinctiveness as it competes alongside other forms of infotainment and recedes into the broader world of communications. And even our "serious" news, espe-cially on television, is dominated by interviews and commentary, rather than independent reporting and analysis. It is a lot easier and less expensive to invite public officials and talking heads into a studio for an hour than it is to spend weeks identifying and analyz-ing important issues.

So what is the future of journalism? What will it look like? Will we soon witness the demise of hard-copy newspapers and magazines? Will the major television networks get out of the news business? Will journalism be able to fulfill its important social roles, whatever shape it assumes in the years to come?

Although much about the future of journalism is difficult to predict, several things appear clear. One is that the pace will continue to quicken. It took twenty days in 1841 for news of the death of President William Henry Harrison to travel from the East Coast to Los Angeles. In contrast, in 1963, more than two-thirds of Americans learned President Kennedy had been shot within a half hour of his assassination. Today, it is hard to believe two-thirds of Americans would not know of a similarly important event within five minutes. Information makes its way across the globe in an instant, and if journalism does not keep up with the information that underlies it, most people will have little use for journalism.

We are also likely to see increasing specialization and segmentation in journalism—as we have seen with cable television. When distribution was expensive and relatively constrained, news producers generated content with wide appeal. Coverage was broad, and generally sought to avoid offending or turning off large numbers of potential customers. Audiences for new media, and many forms of journalism in particular, will tend to be smaller and more homogeneous.

A less obvious but significant aspect of journalism's future may be an increasing importance of books. The demand for faster reporting will exacerbate the trend toward less comprehensive, analytical coverage in publications produced on a regular basis. This will leave a void for considered, deliberate analysis and prose, likely to be filled by a variety of forms of books. This is already taking place to some extent, as many newspaper reporters use books to present the kind of detailed reporting that is less and less at home in newspapers, and even magazines. Recent examples include books about the Iraq war, terrorism, and 9/11, such as Steve Coll's *Ghost Wars*, James Risen's *State of War*, and Thomas Ricks's *Fiasco*.

I also expect nonprofit organizations to play an increasingly significant role in journalism—by carrying out journalism themselves, as well as by providing financial support for journalism activities. There are already important not-for-profit news organizations, such as National Public Radio and the *Christian Science Monitor*. There are also influential publications affiliated with nonprofit organizations, like *Consumer Reports*, the monthly put out by Consumers Union, and the magazine put out by AARP (formerly known as the American Association of Retired Persons), which bills itself as the "world's largest circulation magazine," shipped to more than twenty million homes of almost forty million members.

As the economics of the news business proves more challenging, there will be a growing need for financial support from sources other than for-profit corporations to fund journalism endeavors. New journalism ventures will be created, and existing non-profits are likely to expand to fill some of the void. The more than $200 million gift to National Public Radio from the estate of McDonald's heiress Joan Kroc certainly will not be the last significant philanthropic contribution aimed at ensuring a viable future for journalism. Just as medicine and the health care sector depend on both private enterprise and philanthropy to survive, it is likely that will eventually become true of journalism as well.

Also clear, of course, is that journalism will be practiced by many more people not employed by traditional news organizations than ever before. But what, exactly, does the future hold for citizen journalism? Will it become the journalism equivalent of spam e-mail, viewed as an unauthentic nuisance? Will it become a kind of "minor leagues" that serves as a breeding ground for a limited number of people talented and determined enough to break into the "big leagues" of professional journalism?

One thing certain about citizen journalism is that it will be diverse. It has already assumed many forms, and addresses a seemingly endless variety of topics.

Citizen journalism also seems certain to persist. It

is exploding because of a convergence of powerful currents propelling its supply and demand. There are needs not being satisfied by established news organizations at the same time many people have things to say, and knowledge to share. Moreover, the strand of citizen journalism featuring collaboration among groups of people is part of a broader phenomenon, described by law professor Yochai Benkler as the emergence of a "networked information economy" in his book *The Wealth of Networks: How Social Production Transforms Markets and Freedom.*

Like traditional journalists and media organizations, individual citizen journalists will ultimately rise or fall based on the reputations they acquire and their ability to foster the trust of the consumers of their products. But citizen journalism as a whole appears very much here to stay.

Citizen journalism is not just a phenomenon unto itself. Evidence suggests that citizen journalism is prompting improvements within traditional media. The fact-checking capacity of bloggers and others on the Web has forced established journalists to redouble their efforts to get things right, lest they be taken to task by readers. Citizen journalism has also impelled traditional news organizations to be more creative, and more responsive to the interests of their audience.

The proliferation of blogs and other Internet publications has also benefited large media organizations by dampening some of the concern and criticism that media consolidation has diminished journalistic independence and limited the number of voices with an outlet to the public.

That citizen journalism is transforming "old" media organizations should not be surprising. Emerging news media change existing ones. Just as television has dramatically impacted print news—particularly with the advent of twenty-four-hour cable news—the dissemination of news through the Internet is transforming, and will continue to transform, print, television, and radio journalism. As surely as "history keeps happening" the "media keep changing," remarks Michael Schudson in *The Sociology of News*.

But will the journalism that emerges in the Internet era be robust enough to fulfill its vital functions in our society? Will the patchwork of traditional news organizations, citizen journalists, and new journalism ventures provide the information we need to make informed decisions as voters and as consumers?

I am hopeful, even though it is hard to imagine exactly how the transformation of journalism will unfold. Will we look back in ten years and view as quaint the way news is generated and consumed today? Remember life before e-mail—less than a decade ago for most of us? Without the Web? Without Google? This seems like another world.

Yet the future of journalism depends not only on how suppliers of news organize themselves, but also on consumers. If people do not demand (and pay for) high-quality news and analysis, we are unlikely to get much of it. We might be well served by more initiatives like the News Literacy program being developed at Stony Brook University in New York, which aims to teach students how to be more discriminating news consumers in the Internet age. With the support of a $1.7 million grant from the Knight Foundation, Stony Brook has committed to teach its News Literacy class, designed for all undergraduates, to more than ten thousand students over a four-year period. In its present incarnation, the course addresses issues like the purposes of press freedom, what a journalist is, and who decides what constitutes news.

While I certainly have my own outlook about these questions—as should be apparent by now—regardless of what specific views students adopt during the course, one result should be an increased interest in quality journalism. If successful, the Stony Brook program could serve as a model for other schools across the country. We need to encourage efforts to reverse the trend among most mainstream news organizations toward less coverage and diminished substance. The best journalism is as good as ever. But we need more of it if the new journalism landscape is going to tell us more of what we *should* know.

## Conclusions

I've written this book because I think journalism is invaluable, not to denigrate it. Ben Bradlee, former editor of the *Washington Post*, who presided over the paper for three decades including during Watergate, recently described journalism as a "holy profession." Although I do not adhere to the view that journalism is limited to professionals, I agree with his sentiment that its importance is of the highest order. At its core, journalism is the way we share information and ideas with our fellow citizens. It is the lifeblood of our political system and an engine for our intellectual vitality. We cannot do without it.

I am not one of those people who believe that "old media" is a dinosaur whose time has come and gone. To the contrary, I am a voracious consumer of old media, and not about to give that up. As for the "new media," much of it is junk. And most of it is not journalism, even properly defined by function rather than affiliation with established media organizations.

Nevertheless, the past century of big-media dominance has featured the development of a pervasive system of preferences for professional journalists that are denied to everyone else. That system is built largely on a view of press liberty that is inconsistent with the Constitution's vision of it as an individual right belonging to a person passing out leaflets on a street corner just as much as to a reporter for the *Wall Street Journal* or *USA Today*. The system of preferences also raises serious questions about whether nonprofessional journalists are being deprived of their rights to equality when they are denied privileges extended to professionals engaged in similar activities. In addition to these problems, this system of preferential treatment will be increasingly strained in the years to come, as the nature of journalism changes, and nonprofessional journalists become more common and more active.

We must adjust our conception of journalism, and the legal framework built upon it, to reflect that there may be journalists who make it their profession, but one need not be a professional journalist to *practice* journalism. Technological and social changes provide an opportunity to recall what we seem to have forgotten—that the First Amendment is for all of us. We are all given the right and the responsibility to share with the world our insights and inspirations.

Forces from within the press and outside it have moved us to the point where it is more difficult than ever to tell who is a journalist, and how "professional" journalists differ from other people engaged in sharing news and opinions with the public. This is not to suggest that there is no sense in which professional journalists collectively differ from nonprofessionals as a whole. For the foreseeable future, the work of professionals as a group is certain to be more reliable and better written than the totality of the work by citizen journalists.

Yet subjective assessments about quality or reliability are not a basis for denying rights and privileges to nonprofessionals. In deciding what preferences to extend to people seeking to share their ideas and information, we ought to focus on their objectives, not their methods, on their activities, not who owns the vehicle they use to reach out to others.

We also must avoid assigning rights and privileges to journalists based on judgments about the importance or quality of their work, or the viewpoints they express. As the Supreme Court has explained, "a responsible press is an undoubtedly desirable goal, but press responsibility is not mandated by the Constitution and like many other virtues, it cannot be legislated."

Any other course is directly at odds with fundamental constitutional principles governing freedom of expression, as developed by the Supreme Court over the course of the past century. Although the Court's interpretation of the First Amendment sometimes distinguishes among *types* of speech, and finds that certain kinds of speech are "less central to the interests of the First Amendment than others," it also has made clear that speech on public issues occupies the "highest rung of the hierarchy of First Amendment values" and is entitled to special protection.

If an individual or organization seeks to disseminate certain information or ideas to the public, it would be dangerous were the government to make itself the arbiter of whether that information or idea is genuinely speech on a public issue, or otherwise judge the relative value of that speech, for purposes of allocating press privileges. Deciding what journalism is worthwhile is akin to what is referred to as "content regulation" of speech, which is strongly disfavored. Content regulation is reviewed by courts under the most exacting standard, generally requiring a compelling reason for disfavoring the speech in question, as well as a "narrowly tailored" fit between that compelling interest and the rule disfavoring the speech. Another central tenet of First Amendment law is the principle that freedom of expression should not depend on the identity of the speaker. Together, these principles make clear that allocating press preferences only or predominantly to those affiliated with traditional news organizations is deeply problematic.

There is no doubt that the institutional media have played an important role over the last century in helping expand the scope of First Amendment rights. They initiated many of the lawsuits that paved the way for the development of broad rights of free expression that benefit all of us. But their efforts do not entitle them to rights unavailable to others engaged in journalism activities. The First Amendment has never been understood to call for such a distinction, nor should it. As for the discretionary privileges conferred by the government—like special rights of access, and exemptions from otherwise generally applicable laws—if there was once a defensible basis for subsidizing and facilitating only the speech of traditional news organizations on the ground that they were the near-exclusive outlet for journalism activities, that rationale grows increasingly dubious, as established news organizations become merely part of the sea of information and ideas exchanged every moment of every day.

It is time to do away with the journalistic caste system we have created, which elevates the employees of established news organizations above other citizens engaged in the practice of journalism. It is time to reclaim the conception of press liberty as a right and a privilege that belongs to all of us, not just mainstream news organizations. It is time to recognize that technology has caught up with the First Amendment and truly made us all journalists now, and to work together in ensuring that the journalism of the twenty-first century enables us to thrive as a society.

# Notes

*page*

1 according to a poll conducted in 2005: Annenberg Public Policy Center Survey (conducted during March and April 2005).

2 The most recent edition of the *New Oxford American Dictionary*: *New Oxford American Dictionary* (2d ed. 2005) (italics added to text).

6 "Freedom of the press": A. J. Liebling, "Do You Belong in Journalism," *New Yorker* (May 14, 1960).

10 "we had a philosophical disagreement": Adam Liptak, "News Media Pay Scientist in Suit," *New York Times* (June 3, 2006) (quoting CNN spokesperson Laurie Goldberg).

11 Polls consistently reflect public dissatisfaction: For discussions of the public's view of the press, see David A.

Yaloff and Kenneth Dautrich, *The First Amendment and the Media in the Court of Public Opinion* (2002); Patrick D. Healy, "Believe It: The Media's Credibility Headache Gets Worse," *New York Times* (May 22, 2005) (reporting poll results showing declining confidence); BBC/Reuters/Media Poll Center, *Trust in the Media* (May 3, 2006) (among U.S. respondents, only 51 percent agreed the media "reports the news accurately," and only 29 percent agreed the media "reports all sides of a story"); We Media-Zogby Interactive Poll (national survey of 5,384 adults conducted between January 30, 2007 and February 1, 2007) (more than 70 percent of respondents "somewhat dissatisfied" or "very dissatisfied" with "the quality of journalism").

11  "We've seen greater skepticism": "Buying Silence," *On the Media* (NPR) (June 9, 2006) (text of radio interview).

12  "The center of thinking": Sue Ellen Christian, "Experts: Students Must Prepare for Future of Citizen Media," *Quill* (August 2006).

13  "society is in the early phases": "Among the Audience: A Survey of New Media," *Economist* (April 22, 2006), p. 19.

13  "Who Killed the Newspaper?": *Economist* (August 24, 2006).

13  "Journalism as we know it": Geneva Overholser, *On Behalf of Journalism: A Manifesto for Change* (2006).

13  The October 2005 issue: Jon Marshall, "Citizen Journalism Continues to Surge," *Quill* (October 2005).

14  "students must prepare": Sue Ellen Christian, "Experts: Students Must Prepare for Future of Citizen Media," *Quill* (August 2006).

17  "objectivity seemed a natural": Michael Schudson, *The Sociology of News* (2003), p. 82.

21  "too little news in the news": Leonard Downie and Robert Kaiser, *The News About the News: American Journalism in Peril* (2003), p. 273.

21  "the drift away from serious coverage": Ibid., p. 243.

22  "new danger is that": Bill Kovach and Tom Rosenstiel, *The Elements of Journalism* (2001), p. 18.

22  "mega-corporations that have taken over": Tom Fenton, *Bad News: The Decline of Reporting, the Business of News, and the Danger to Us All* (2005), p. 11. Fenton explores the role of diminished news reporting in facilitating the 9/11 attacks, specifically considering how increased public awareness of the threat might have prevented the disaster (pp. 1–9).

22  "The economic imperatives": Bruce W. Sanford, *Don't Shoot the Messenger: How Our Growing Hatred of the Media Threatens Free Speech for All of Us* (1999), pp. 8–9.

23  "quiet consumers' boycott of the press": James Fallows, *Breaking the News: How the Media Undermine American Democracy* (1997), p. 3.

23  *The Daily Show with Jon Stewart*: J. R. Fox, G. Koloen, and V. Sahin, "No Joke: An Examination of *The Daily Show with Jon Stewart* and Broadcast Television Networks as 2004 Presidential Election Campaign Information Sources." Forthcoming in *Journal of Broadcasting and Electronic Media*.

24  More recently injected into this mix are the Internet and the Web: Although often used interchangeably, the Internet and the Web are not synonymous. The Internet is often described as a collection of intercon-

nected computer networks that operate under standardized protocols. The Internet's origins date back to the 1950s, when work on its predecessor systems began under the auspices of the United States government. The Web is a collection of interconnected documents and other resources, accessible *through* the Internet, developed decades after the Internet, by Tim Berners-Lee according to most accounts. Lee's book *Weaving the Web: The Original Design and Ultimate Destiny of the World Wide Web* (2000) offers his own account of the Web's creation.

25 *Business Week* reported: "Blogs Will Change Your Business," *Business Week* (May 2, 2005).

26 According to a 2005 survey: America Online survey (September 16, 2005).

26 This sentiment appears: Pew Internet & American Life Project, *Bloggers: A Portrait of the Internet's New Storytellers* (July 19, 2006).

26 It is also evident from polling during January and February 2007: We Media-Zogby Interactive Poll (national survey of 5,384 adults conducted between January 30, 2007 and February 1, 2007).

29 There are already numerous other "hyperlocal" Web sites set up across the country: In early 2007, J-Lab: The Institute of Interactive Journalism, at the Philip Merrill College of Journalism, University of Maryland, produced a useful survey of citizen media and "hyperlocal" ventures, *Citizen Media: Fad or the Future of News?*, available at the Knight Citizen News Network Web site.

31 "The Internet made this story": Michael Kinsley, "In Defense of Matt Drudge," *Time* (February 2, 1998).

32  More than fifty million Americans: Pew Internet & American Life Project, *Online News* (March 22, 2006).

32  39 percent of Internet users: Pew Internet & American Life Project, *Bloggers: A Portrait of the Internet's New Storytellers* (July 19, 2006).

32  According to another, from early 2007: We Media-Zogby Interactive Poll (national survey of 5,384 adults conducted between January 30, 2007 and February 1, 2007) (more than 74 percent of respondents said "citizen journalism" is "very important" or "somewhat important" to the "future of journalism").

33  According to a study conducted by the University of Pennsylvania: Annenberg Public Policy Center Survey (conducted between March and May 2005).

33  an informal poll of readers: Randy Dotinga, "Are Bloggers Journalists? Do They Deserve Press Protections?," *Christian Science Monitor* (February 2, 2005).

36  "there is not much relation": Nicholas Lemann, "Amateur Hour: Journalism Without Journalists," *New Yorker* (August 7, 2006).

36  "forms part of a larger attempt": Samuel Freedman, "PublicEye," cbsnews.com (March 31, 2006).

36  "new and accurate information": Fred Brown, " 'Citizen' Journalism Is Not Professional Journalism," *Quill* (August 2005).

37  "make up the rules as they go": Andrew Kantor, "Technology Empowers Amateur Journalism—For Better or Worse," *USA Today* (September 7, 2006).

37  "the legitimate gripe": Richard A. Posner, "Bad News," *New York Times Book Review* (July 31, 2005).

39  filed a lawsuit in a California state court: *Apple Com-*

*puter, Inc. v. Doe 1,* No. 1-04-CV-032178, Superior Court, Santa Clara, CA (March 11, 2005).

41  In a widely anticipated ruling: *O'Grady v. Superior Court of Santa Clara County* (Cal. Ct. Appeals, May 26, 2006).

42  did not appeal the ruling: Apple was later ordered by the trial court to pay more than $700,000 to the lawyers who represented the Web sites against Apple's attempt to force them to reveal their sources, with the court noting that by successfully resisting Apple's efforts "a significant benefit" had been conferred "on all journalists, the free press, and on the general public as a whole."

45  Journalism has been elegantly described: James Carey, "The Press, Public Opinion, and Public Discourse: On the Edge of the Postmodern" in Eve Stryker Munson and Catherine A. Warren, eds., *James Carey: A Critical Reader* (1997).

CHAPTER 2: THE PRESS AND THE PUBLIC
UNDER THE CONSTITUTION

*page*

48  According to an annual survey: First Amendment Center, State of the First Amendment Survey 2006. See also David A. Yaloff and Kenneth Dautrich, *The First Amendment and the Media in the Court of Public Opinion* (2002), p. 47.

48  James Madison believed: Letter from James Madison to W. T. Barry (August 4, 1822).

48  This view: For discussions of the structural model, see C. Edwin Baker, *Media, Markets, and Democracy* (2002), p. 195. ("The only obvious reason that the

press merits constitutional protection from democratic processes is that this protection is thought to serve its role in that democratic arrangement."); David T. Z. Mindich, *Tuned Out: Why Americans Under 40 Don't Follow the News* (2005), p. 15; Lee C. Bollinger, *Images of Free Press* (1991), p. 1 (calling it the "central image" of the press); Leonard W. Levy, *Emergence of a Free Press* (1985), p. 273 ("the press enjoyed a preferred position in the American constitutional scheme because of its special relationship to popular government"); Herbert J. Gans, *Democracy and the News* (2003), p. 21 ("As a profession, journalism views itself as supporting and strengthening the roles of citizens in democracy.").

49 "the highest rung": Lee C. Bollinger, *Images of Free Press* (1991), p. 57.

50 "the primary purpose": William J. Brennan, Jr., October 17, 1979 Address, published in 32 *Rutgers L. Rev.* 173, 176 (1979).

54 "those who called for": Anthony Lewis, "A Preferred Position for Journalism?," 7 *Hofstra L. Rev.* 595, 597 (1979).

55 In fact, in 1951: *Dennis v. United States,* 341 U.S. 494, 503 (1951) (citing *Schenck v. United States,* 249 U.S. 47 [1919]).

59 One of the most forceful arguments: Justice Stewart's speech was later memorialized in an article. Potter Stewart, "Or of the Press," 26 *Hastings L. J.* 631 (1974/1975).

60 In fact, Stewart never went quite as far: In 1974, Justice Stewart wrote the proposition that "the Constitution imposes upon government the affirmative duty to

make available to journalists sources of information not available to the public generally . . . finds no support in the words of the Constitution or in any decision of this Court." *Pell v. Procunier,* 417 U.S. 817, 834–35 (1974). He did author several opinions, however, in which he disagreed with the approach of a majority of the Court in cases involving the press, and would have decided them in a way more protective of press interests. See, e.g., *Zurcher v. Stanford Daily,* 436 U.S. 547, 570 (1978) (Stewart, J., dissenting); *Houchins v. KQED, Inc.,* 438 U.S. 1, 16–19 (1978) (Stewart, J., concurring) (arguing that the concept of equal access for the public and the press "must be accorded more flexibility in order to accommodate the practical distinctions between the press and the general public").

60 the Court repeatedly described freedom of the press: Decisions describing freedom of the press as a "personal" right include *Gitlow v. New York,* 268 U.S. 652, 666 (1925); *Near v. Minnesota,* 283 U.S. 697, 707 (1931); *Lovell v. Griffin,* 303 U.S. 444, 450 (1938).

60 For example, in 1938: *Lovell v. Griffin,* 303 U.S. 444, 451 (1938).

61 In deciding a libel case in 1967: *Curtis Publishing Co. v. The Associated Press,* 388 U.S. 130, 149 (1967).

61 It was in 1972: *Branzburg v. Hayes,* 408 U.S. 665 (1972).

66 "informed public opinion": *Pittsburgh Press Co. v. Pittsburgh Commission on Human Relations,* 413 U.S. 376, 382 (1973) (quoting *Grosjean v. American Press Co.,* 297 U.S. 233, 250 [1936]).

66 In a 1965 ruling: *Estes v. Texas,* 381 U.S. 532, 539 (1965).

66 A year later: *Mills v. Alabama,* 384 U.S. 214, 219 (1966).

66 A 1983 decision: *Minneapolis Star and Tribune Co. v. Minnesota Commissioner of Revenue,* 460 U.S. 575, 585 (1983).

67 The Court's approach is exemplified: *First National Bank of Boston v. Bellotti,* 435 U.S. 765, 781–82 (1978).

68 As a general matter: The proposition that the United States Supreme Court is the ultimate arbiter of meaning of the federal Constitution is necessarily an oversimplification of a complicated issue. For a more detailed discussion of my views, see "Judicial Supremacy and Nonjudicial Interpretation of the Constitution," 24 *Hastings Constitutional L. Q.* 359 (1997).

69 Within a mere five years: *Silkwood v. Kerr-McGee Corp.,* 563 F.2d 433, 437 (10th Cir. 1977).

69 One of the Court's justices: *In re Roche,* 448 U.S. 1312 (1980) (Brennan, J.) (reviewing application for stay of enforcement pending review of state court order finding journalist in civil contempt for refusal to disclose identity of sources).

70 In 2003: *McKevitt v. Pallasch,* 339 F.3d 530, 532 (7th Cir. 2003).

75 "done a great service": Mark Fainaru-Wada and Lance Williams, *Game of Shadows* (2007), pp. 284–85.

76 "what's past is prologue": William Shakespeare, *The Tempest,* Act 2, Scene 1.

78 a decision involving an employee of the World Championship Wrestling: *In re Madden,* 151 F.3d 125 (3d Cir. 1998).

80 Several leading First Amendment scholars: The First

Amendment scholars advancing a view of the Press Clause as protecting the "institutional press" include Frederick Schauer, "Towards an Institutional First Amendment," 89 *Minnesota L. Rev.* 1256 (2005), and David A. Anderson, "Freedom of the Press in Wartime," 77 *University of Colorado L. Rev.* 49 (2006). See also Randall P. Bezanson, "The New Free Press Guarantee," 63 *Virginia L. Rev.* 731, 734 (1977) (Press Clause is designed to safeguard "institutional" independence).

81 "primarily as a protector": David A. Anderson, "Freedom of the Press in Wartime," 77 *University of Colorado L. Rev.* 49, 95 (2006).

81 Chief Justice Warren Burger recognized this: *First National Bank of Boston v. Bellotti,* 435 U.S. 765, 799 (1978) (Burger, C. J., concurring).

83 "the press is entitled": Floyd Abrams, "The Press *Is* Different: Reflections on Justice Stewart and the Autonomous Press," 7 *Hofstra L. Rev.* 563, 570, 572, 580 (1978/1979).

83 "does not 'belong'": *First National Bank of Boston v. Bellotti,* 435 U.S. 765, 802 (1978) (Burger, C. J., concurring).

84 "the very task of including": *First National Bank of Boston v. Bellotti,* 435 U.S. 765, 801 (1978) (Burger, C. J., concurring).

84 "in a very real sense": Jon Paul Dilts, "The Press Clause and Press Behavior: Revisiting the Implications of Citizenship," 7 *Communications Law and Policy* 25, 34 (2002).

84 "If the courts extend": *In re Grand Jury Subpoena,* 438 F.3d 1141, 1158 (D.C. Cir. 2006) (Sentelle, J., concurring).

86 "the purpose of the Constitution": *Pennekamp v. Florida*, 328 U.S. 331, 364 (1946) (Frankfurter, J., concurring).

## CHAPTER 3: THE PRIORITY OF THE PRESS
*page*

92 The archive sued: *National Security Archive v. U.S. Department of Defense*, 880 F.2d 1381, 1387 (D.C. Cir. 1989).

99 Back in the 1970s: *Consumers Union v. Periodical Correspondents Assoc.*, 515 F.2d 1341 (D.C. Cir. 1975).

100 Adhering to that ruling: *Schreibman v. Holmes*, 203 F.3d 53, 199 WL 963070 (D.C. Cir. 1999).

105 "It is the press corps' briefing room": Katherine Q. Seelye, "White House Approves Pass for Blogger," *New York Times* (March 7, 2005) (noting issuance of day pass to blogger Garrett M. Graff, editor of Fish-bowlDC).

115 The government opposed her efforts: *In re Grand Jury Proceedings*, No. 01-20745 (5th Cir. August 17, 2001).

119 lawsuit brought by former University of Alabama football head coach Mike Price: *Price v. Time, Inc.*, 416 F.3d 1327 (11th Cir. 2005).

123 In one case, filed two decades ago: *Jersawitz v. Hanberry*, 783 F.2d 1532 (11th Cir. 1986).

124 A year later, a different appeals court: *Storer Communications, Inc. v. Giovan*, 810 F.2d 580 (6th Cir. 1987).

131 "Journalism and a free press": Lee C. Bollinger, "Statement on the Future of Journalism Education" (April 2003).

132  One court determined: *Von Bulow v. Von Bulow,* 811 F.2d 136, 144 (2d Cir. 1987).

133  Another similarly found: *Schoen v. Schoen,* 5 F.3d 1289, 1293 (9th Cir. 1993).

CHAPTER 4: THE TRANSFORMATION OF JOURNALISM AND THE CITIZEN JOURNALISTS' BATTLE FOR EQUALITY

*page*

140  2 percent of its registered contributors: Stacy Schiff, "Know It All: Can Wikipedia Conquer Expertise?" *New Yorker* (July 31, 2006).

142  "envisions many tiers": Sue Ellen Christian, "Experts: Students Must Prepare for Future of Citizen Media," *Quill* (August 2006).

144  "We're in the middle of a revolution": Kim Peterson, "News Brought to You by the Average Joe," *Seattle Times* (September 27, 2006).

145  the "voice of God": Jay Rosen, PressThink (September 20, 2006).

146  In another important early victory: *O'Grady v. Superior Court of Santa Clara County* (Cal. Ct. Appeals, May 26, 2006).

147  Mark Nickolas: Nickolas also filed a lawsuit in July 2006 against the Kentucky governor and other state officials, challenging the constitutionality of the state's policy blocking state employees' access to his and other political blogs.

148  The *Sun*'s lawsuit: *Baltimore Sun Co. v. Ehrlich,* 437 F.3d 410 (4th Cir. 2006).

150  "deciding who would qualify": David A. Anderson,

"Freedom of the Press in Wartime," 77 *University of Colorado L. Rev.* 49, 68 (2006).

151 "when older news media": David T. Z. Mindich, *Just the Facts: How "Objectivity" Came to Define American Journalism* (1998), p. 2.

156 "a solution in search of a problem": Zachary Coile, "Senator Leads Drive for Federal Media Shield Law," *San Francisco Chronicle* (September 21, 2006) (quoting Deputy Attorney General Paul McNulty).

159 "don't represent the public": Ken Auletta, "Fortress Bush," *New Yorker* (January 19, 2004).

159 "You're making a huge assumption": Ibid.

161 "serious failing": Dick Thornburgh, "Doctors, Lawyers, Priests—And Journalists?," *Wall Street Journal* (July 3, 2006) (italics added to text).

163 "The day may come": "Media Sources Need a Shield," *Los Angeles Times* (June 6, 2006) (editorial).

164 "the people who invented this country": Letter from Bill Keller on the *Times*'s Banking Records Report, *New York Times* (June 25, 2006).

165 "all the news that's fit to print": The slogan of the *New York Times,* which, according to the *Times,* was coined by owner Adolph S. Ochs himself in 1896 after a contest found no stronger candidate. The phrase first appeared on the editorial page of the paper, and then moved to its current front-page location on February 10, 1897.

165 "news is not a mirror of reality": Michael Schudson, *The Sociology of News* (2003), p. 33.

165 "The notion of journalism": Robert W. McChesney, *The Problem of the Media: U.S. Communications Politics in the 21st Century* (2004), p. 87.

168 "The era of hegemonic networks": David Remnick, "Nattering Nabobs," *New Yorker* (July 10, 2006).

170 "a commercial product": James T. Hamilton, *All the News That's Fit to Sell: How the Market Transforms Information into News* (2004), p. 37.

CHAPTER 5: A WORLD IN WHICH WE'RE ALL JOURNALISTS

*page*

179 "if everybody's entitled": Josh Gerstein, "Bloggers Blur the Definition of Reporters' Privilege," *New York Sun* (December 6, 2004).

179 "institutional agnosticism": Frederick Schauer, "Towards an Institutional First Amendment," 89 *Minnesota L. Rev.* 1256, 1272 (2005).

184 "political institutions and media institutions": Michael Schudson, *The Sociology of News* (2003), pp. 54, 154.

184 "the historical relationship": Donald A. Ritchie, *Press Gallery: Congress and the Washington Correspondents* (1991), p. 1.

184 "The news media can be": Timothy E. Cook, *Governing with the News: The News Media as a Political Institution* (1998), p. 179.

185 "stunning gaps": W. Lance Bennett and William Serrin, "The Watchdog Role," in Geneva Overholser and Kathleen Hall Jamieson, eds., *Institutions of American Democracy: The Press* (2005), p. 169.

185 "parajournalists": Michael Schudson, *The Sociology of News* (2003), p. 3.

186 As renowned publisher: W. A. Swanberg, *Pulitzer* (1967), p. 51.

186　The Supreme Court seemed to recognize this: *Reno v. ACLU,* 521 U.S. 844, 870 (1997).

187　As the Court also noted: *Talley v. California,* 362 U.S. 60, 64 (1960).

187　More recently, in striking down: *McIntyre v. Ohio Elections Commission,* 514 U.S. 334, 342 (1995).

197　"networked information economy": Yochai Benkler, *The Wealth of Networks: How Social Production Transforms Markets and Freedom* (2006).

198　"history keeps happening": Michael Schudson, *The Sociology of News* (2003), p. 90.

200　"holy profession": *Free Speech: Jim Lehrer with Ben Bradlee* (PBS) (June 19, 2006) (text of television interview).

202　"a responsible press": *Miami Herald Publishing Co. v. Tornillo,* 418 U.S. 241, 256 (1974).

202　"less central to the interests": *Dun & Bradstreet, Inc. v. Greenmoss Builders, Inc.,* 472 U.S. 749, 759 n.5 (1985).

# Bibliography

Abrams, Floyd. *Speaking Freely: Trials of the First Amendment*. New York: Viking, 2005.

Auletta, Ken. *Backstory: Inside the Business of News*. New York: Penguin, 2003.

Bagdikian, Ben H. *The New Media Monopoly*. Boston: Beacon, 2004.

Baker, C. Edwin. *Media, Markets, and Democracy*. New York: Cambridge University Press, 2002.

Benkler, Yochai. *The Wealth of Networks: How Social Production Transforms Markets and Freedom*. New Haven: Yale University Press, 2006.

Bezanson, Randall P. *How Free Can the Press Be?* Chicago: University of Illinois Press, 2003.

Bollinger, Lee C. *Images of Free Press*. Chicago: University of Chicago Press, 1991.

Briggs, Asa, and Peter Burke. *A Social History of the Media: From Gutenberg to the Internet.* 2d ed. Malden, Massachusetts: Polity, 2005.

Burns, Eric. *Infamous Scribblers: The Founding Fathers and the Rowdy Beginnings of American Journalism.* New York: PublicAffairs, 2006.

Carey, James W. *Communication as Culture: Essays on Media and Society.* New York: Routledge, 1992.

Cater, Douglass. *The Fourth Branch of Government.* New York: Vintage, 1959.

Cook, Timothy E. *Governing with the News: The News Media as a Political Institution.* Chicago: University of Chicago Press, 1998.

Cook, Timothy E., ed. *Freeing the Presses: The First Amendment in Action.* Baton Rouge: Louisiana State University Press, 2005.

De Zengotita, Thomas. *Mediated: How the Media Shapes Your World and the Way You Live in It.* New York: Bloomsbury, 2005.

Downie, Leonard, and Robert Kaiser. *The News About the News: American Journalism in Peril.* New York: Vintage, 2003.

Fallows, James. *Breaking the News: How the Media Undermine American Democracy.* New York: Vintage, 1997.

Fenton, Tom. *Bad News: The Decline of Reporting, the Business of News, and the Danger to Us All.* New York: Regan, 2005.

Gans, Herbert J. *Democracy and the News.* New York: Oxford University Press, 2003.

Gillmor, Dan. *We the Media: Grassroots Journalism by the People, for the People.* Sebastopol, California: O'Reilly, 2004.

Gleason, Timothy W. *The Watchdog Concept: The Press and the Courts in Nineteenth Century America*. Ames: Iowa State University Press, 1990.

Gleick, James. *Faster: The Acceleration of Just About Everything*. New York: Pantheon, 1999.

Hamilton, James T. *All the News That's Fit to Sell: How the Market Transforms Information into News*. Princeton: Princeton University Press, 2004.

Jamieson, Kathleen Hall, and Paul Waldman. *The Press Effect: Politicians, Journalists, and the Stories That Shape the Political World*. New York: Oxford University Press, 2003.

Jenkins, Henry. *Convergence Culture: Where Old and New Media Collide*. New York: New York University Press, 2006.

Kovach, Bill, and Tom Rosenstiel. *The Elements of Journalism*. New York: Three Rivers, 2001.

Levy, Leonard W. *Emergence of a Free Press*. Chicago: Ivan R. Dee, 1985.

Lewis, Anthony. *Make No Law: The Sullivan Case and the First Amendment*. New York: Vintage, 1992.

Lippmann, Walter. *Public Opinion*. New York: Free Press, 1977. (Originally published 1922.)

Martin, Robert W. T. *The Free and Open Press: The Founding of American Democratic Press Liberty, 1640–1800*. New York: New York University Press, 2001.

McChesney, Robert W. *The Problem of the Media: U.S. Communications Politics in the 21st Century*. New York: Monthly Review, 2004.

McChesney, Robert W., and Ben Scott, eds. *Our Unfree Press: 100 Years of Radical Media Criticism*. New York: New Press, 2004.

Mindich, David T. Z. *Just the Facts: How "Objectivity" Came to Define American Journalism.* New York: New York University Press, 1998.

———. *Tuned Out: Why Americans Under 40 Don't Follow the News.* New York: Oxford University Press, 2005.

Novick, Peter. *That Noble Dream: The "Objectivity Question" and the American Historical Profession.* New York: Cambridge University Press, 1988.

Overholser, Geneva. *On Behalf of Journalism: A Manifesto for Change.* Annenberg Public Policy Center. http://www.annenbergpublicpolicycenter.org/Overholser/20061011_JournStudy.pdf [October 11, 2006].

Overholser, Geneva, and Kathleen Hall Jamieson, eds. *Institutions of American Democracy: The Press.* New York: Oxford University Press, 2005.

Rabban, David M. *Free Speech in Its Forgotten Years, 1870–1920.* New York: Cambridge University Press, 1997.

Reynolds, Glenn. *An Army of Davids: How Markets and Technology Empower Ordinary People to Beat Big Media, Big Government and Other Goliaths.* Nashville: Nelson Current, 2006.

Ritchie, Donald A. *Press Gallery: Congress and the Washington Correspondents.* Cambridge: Harvard University Press, 1991.

———. *Reporting from Washington: The History of the Washington Press Corps.* New York: Oxford University Press, 2005.

Rosen, Jay. *What Are Journalists For?* New Haven: Yale University Press, 1999.

Sanford, Bruce W. *Don't Shoot the Messenger: How Our*

*Growing Hatred of the Media Threatens Free Speech for All of Us*. Lanham, Maryland: Rowman & Littlefield, 1999.

Schudson, Michael. *The Sociology of News*. New York: Norton, 2003.

Schwartz, Barry. *The Paradox of Choice: Why More Is Less*. New York: HarperCollins, 2004.

Starr, Paul. *The Creation of the Media: Political Origins of Modern Communications*. New York: Basic, 2004.

Stephens, Mitchell. *A History of News*. 3d ed. New York: Oxford University Press, 2007.

Stone, Geoffrey R. *Perilous Times: Free Speech in Wartime*. New York: Norton, 2004.

Sunstein, Cass R. *Democracy and the Problem of Free Speech*. New York: Free Press, 1995.

Thomas, Helen. *Watchdogs of Democracy?: The Waning Washington Press Corps and How It Has Failed the Public*. New York: Scribner, 2006.

Weaver, David H., Randal A. Beam, Bonnie J. Brownlee, Paul S. Voakes, and G. Cleveland Wilhoit. *The American Journalist in the 21st Century: U.S. News People at the Dawn of a New Millennium*. Mahwah, New Jersey: Lawrence Erlbaum Associates, 2007.

Yaloff, David A., and Kenneth Dautrich. *The First Amendment and the Media in the Court of Public Opinion*. New York: Cambridge University Press, 2002.

# Index

## About the Author

Scott Gant is an attorney in Washington, D.C., where his practice includes constitutional and media law. He is former counsel for *The New Republic* and a graduate of Harvard Law School.

Printed in the United States
By Bookmasters